Contents

Rare Lilies of California

Catherine M. Watters

Peggy Lee Fiedler

Rare Lilies of California

PEGGY LEE FIEDLER

Illustrations by

CATHERINE M. WATTERS

CALIFOR   SOCIETY

Dedicated to our fathers

CALIFORNIA NATIVE PLANT SOCIETY
EXECUTIVE COUNCIL, 1996
Lori Hubbart, President
Joan Stewart, V.P., Administration
Bob Berka, V.P., Finance
Ray Butler, V.P., Legislation
Jim Shevock, V.P., Plant Programs
Michael and Lynn Lindsay, V.P., Education
Phyllis M. Faber, V.P., Publications
David Magney, V.P., Conservation
Randi McCormick, V.P., Chapter Relations
Jake Sigg, Recording Secretary

PUBLICATIONS COMMITTEE, 1996
Phyllis M. Faber, Chairman
Wilma Follette
Joyce Hawley
Elly Bade
Carol Baird
Harlan Kessel
Barbara Malloch Leitner
Catherine Cort
Greg Jirak
Steve Hartman
Bob Berka

Cover and book design by Beth Hansen

Printed in Hong Kong through Global Interprint, Petaluma, California

ISBN: 0-943460-30-1

Library of Congress Catalog Card Number: 96-086098

This book was set in Melencolia Titling, Berthold Script, and Horley Old Style.

Color Plates

Foreword

Among the thousands of plant species found in the state of California, about half of them nowhere else, the lilies are outstandingly beautiful and interesting elements. Anyone who has seen mariposa lilies growing up through the dry grass and flowering in late spring or summer, enjoyed the beauties of rare fritillarias on their clay, serpentine, or other unusual substrates, or who has marveled at the glories of any member of the genus *Lilium* gracing a meadow or roadside cannot but be deeply fascinated with the beauty of these plants and with the starbursts of color and fragrance that they add to their habitats.

We know very little about the biology of most plant species, rare ones being no exception. Specifically, we have just begun to understand the patterns of rarity and the reasons *why* individual plant species are rare. Studying the geographically restricted members of a single plant family as diverse and interesting as the Liliaceae, for a particular geographical region, will provide important ecological and evolutionary insights into how the particular patterns that exist have evolved and why they are maintained.

In this delightful and well-illustrated book, Peggy Lee Fiedler provides the first account of all of the rare species, subspecies, and varieties within a large and broadly circumscribed family of California's plants. Despite its brevity, this book clearly indicates that many native lilies in California are rare, most have no state or federal protection, and virtually all are threatened with local extirpation or extinction. Because of the clear picture that it presents, this work should serve to inspire conservation efforts for the lilies and other plants of California.

Dr. Fiedler has presented a valuable gift to the people of California, and to all those who care about its remarkable native flora. For that reason, it will be studied, for education and enjoyment, by many. I am delighted to be able to commend it enthusiastically for these purposes.

Peter H. Raven

Preface

I wanted to write this book for several reasons. Although much has been said about rarity in plants, it has not been synthesized or summarized for any major group of related plant species. Oversimplifications have been offered to lay botanists, and little ecological or evolutionary context about the biology of rarity has been provided to professionals. Oversimplification could be remedied by a clear text that omits the use of arcane botanical jargon, but context would be more elusive. I believe that using a well-known plant family, such as the Liliaceae *sensu lato*, to illustrate the many complex and contextual facets of rarity offers the greatest rewards. Lilies are an extraordinarily diverse group of plants, occurring world-wide in a bewildering array of forms. Lilies also have their own breath-taking aesthetic, one with universal appeal. Finally, lilies are taxonomically complex, with various experts including or excluding different species in the family. Here I have chosen to adopt the latest vision of the family Liliaceae offered by the recently revised *Jepson Manual: Higher Plants of California* (Hickman 1993). Importantly, taxonomic complexity suggests evolutionary complexity, revealing an array of causes and consequences of rarity. Thus, I have also written a brief text on rarity in plants and provided a broad context for this biological phenomenon with rare lilies found in California. May the reader come to appreciate the uniqueness of our California flora, gain greater insight into its extraordinary taxa, and ultimately, work toward the preservation and restoration of our rare lilies.

Peggy Lee Fiedler
San Francisco, California

Acknowledgments

We wish to thank a great many people for their advice, encouragement, and patience. The University of California Botanic Garden, Berkeley, particularly the former director, Dr. Margaret Race, and Ms. Holly Forbes, provided us unlimited access to their extensive California plant collection, and we gratefully acknowledge their logistical support. Dr. Steve Edwards, Director of the Tilden Botanic Garden, East Bay Regional Parks District, also was helpful in providing an open invitation to the Park District's botanical garden collection. Several present and former staff botanists of the Plant Conservation Program, Natural Heritage Division, California Department of Fish and Game, particularly Ken Berg, Michael Golden, and Diane Ikeda, provided us with color slides and collecting permits for the rare lilies. The California Native Plant Society provided additional color slides for use in preparation of the illustrations. We also are indebted to several individuals who provided us with slides from their personal collections. In this regard we thank Ms. Jeanette Sainz and Dr. Mark Skinner who are as deeply generous as they are skilled in photography. Dr. Dale McNeal, University of the Pacific, graciously provided several *Allium* specimens for depiction. Ms. Phyllis Faber and the California Native Plant Society have patiently assisted us in numerous ways to see this book to completion, and their aesthetic sense and expertise is indelibly seen throughout. Drs. Bruce Pavlik and Dieter Wilken transformed the text with their characteristically insightful and thoughtful reviews. Drs. Dale McNeal and Mark Skinner also made many helpful suggestions for a readable text. Any errors in the interpretation of the evolution, ecology, or morphological characteristics of California lilies are those of PLF. The Heckard Fellowship at the Jepson Herbarium, University of California, Berkeley, provided support funds to PLF during the final stages of this project. Finally, we thank Robert, Garrett, and Jena, and Bob, Christopher, and David for their love and generosity of spirit.

Chapter 1

Much has been written about the extraordinary diversity of the California flora. Indeed, it is difficult to add new superlatives to describe plants that attract and captivate botanists who come from around the globe. The richness of the California flora is attributed in part to its annual dicot flora, for example, as exemplified by the profusion of species within the Sunflower family (Asteraceae). Magnificent "living fossils," such as the Coast redwood (*Sequoia sempervirens*) and Bristlecone pine (*Pinus longaeva*), also contribute to the wealth of California plant life. Less well appreciated, perhaps, is the rich petaloid monocot flora. In this regard, the Lily family (Liliaceae) stands alone in the western United States in its long evolutionary history, morphological diversity, phylogenetic complexity, potential economic value, and its singular beauty.

California supports thirty-four native genera of Liliaceae. This is a remarkable number because the Hawaiian flora boasts only nine genera in the family. The entire northeastern United States and adjacent parts of Canada support a comparable forty-one genera, but only within an area ten times as large as California. Thus California should be recognized as an area of monocot richness, even without adding grasses, sedges, orchids, and rushes to the tally. This richness is largely the result of contributions from two sources. First, many genera widespread across the temperate regions of North America are represented in the state by one or a few species. False solomon's seal (*Smilacina racemosa*) is an excellent example. Second, a few genera, such as the mariposa lilies (*Calochortus*), onions (*Allium*), and brodiaeas (*Brodiaea*), are rich in species and infraspecific taxa. These lilies are characteristic of most regions of California, and indeed, serve symbolically to illustrate California's unique botanical history. The new *Jepson Manual: Higher Plants of California* (Hickman 1993), for example, has portrayed the Mount Diablo fairy lantern (*Calochortus pulchellus*) emblazoned on its cover.

W H A T   M A K E S   A   L I L Y   A   L I L Y ?

The traditional family Liliaceae is a large, heterogeneous aggregation, and one of approximately fifteen families traditionally included within the order Liliales. This large and fluid order includes nearly 8000 species distributed worldwide. Approximately one-half of those species belong to the family Liliaceae. However, most botanists today view the lily family less broadly, and have separated many smaller families from the Liliaceae. For example, researchers recognize the Agavaceae, Amaryllidaceae, Calochortaceae, Dracaenaceae, Smilacaceae, and Trilliaceae, among others, as families distinct from the Liliaceae. In particular, the Agavaceae and Amaryllidaceae are often distinguished and contain several hundred taxa each. Thus, it is somewhat more practical to recognize these families as separate and distinct from the true lilies. In fact, most knowledgeable taxonomists recognize these plant families, although their boundaries continue to be debated as to their evolutionary and taxonomic significance. Appendix A illustrates the more recent taxonomic limits of the lilies and their allies. The *Jepson Manual: Higher Plants of California* (Hickman 1993), however, is conservative in its approach to family circumscription, and includes these often-recognized monocot families within the Liliaceae.

The Lily family includes monocots distinguished generally from other petaloid monocots by (1) the presence of bulbs as the underground perennating organ; (2) simple, entire leaves arranged either alternately along the stem or in a basal whorl; (3) showy, undifferentiated "tepals"—i.e., both perianth whorls; (4) six stamens; and (5) a superior ovary with a style that often bears three lobes. California lilies, however, exhibit great variation within this general pattern. For example, the underground stem can be a rhizome (e.g., *Asphodelphus, Clintonia, Scolipus*), corm (e.g., *Androstephium, Bloomeria, Brodiaea, Muilla*), bulb (e.g., *Allium, Calochortus, Camassia, Chlorogalum*), or tuber-like caudex (e.g., *Agave, Leucocrinum, Smilax*). The above-ground stem is either an erect, simple, herbaceous stem (e.g., *Fritillaria, Hesperocallis, Lilium*), or a branching, tree-like stem (e.g., *Nolina, Yucca*). Leaves can either alternate along the stem (e.g., *Disporum, Streptopus*), be arranged in whorls along the stem (e.g., *Fritillaria, Lilium*), or be basally whorled (e.g., *Chlorogalum, Clintonia, Hastingsia*).

The lily perianth most commonly consists of six similar tepals in two whorls of three (e.g., *Lilium, Brodiaea, Dichelostemma*), or less commonly, six tepals in two different whorls of three—the outer "sepals" and the inner "petals" (e.g., *Calochortus, Trillium*). The male flower parts (androecium) typically consist of six fertile stamens (e.g., *Erythronium*), or as three fertile stamens and three sterile staminodia (e.g., *Brodiaea*), or as six fused filaments with lobes between anthers (e.g., *Androstephium*). The female flower parts (gynoecium) generally consist of a superior ovary with a simple, entire stigma (e.g., *Streptopus*), but can also be a superior ovary with a sessile, three-lobed stigma (e.g., *Calochortus*), a superior ovary with six prominent crests and three-lobed stigma (e.g., *Allium* spp.), or a partly inferior ovary and three-lobed stigma (e.g., *Stenanthium*). The fruit is either a capsule (e.g., *Odontostomum, Tofieldia, Triteleia*), berry (e.g., *Clintonia, Smilacina, Smilax*), or berry-like capsule (e.g., *Trillium*). Figure 1.1 illustrates some of the great morphological variation that can be found in California's lilies.

LILIACEOUS GENERA IN CALIFORNIA

Forty liliaceous genera are found in the California flora. Six (*Aloe, Asparagus, Asphodelus, Ipheion, Muscari,* and *Nothoscordum*) are wholly exotic to the state, while *Allium* has both native and exotic species (Appendix B). In total, 248 taxa within the Liliaceae are found in California, only eleven (or 4%) of which are considered non-native species.

Other patterns of the California lilies are of general interest. For example, eleven genera (*Androstephium, Hesperocallis, Leucocrinum, Maianthemum, Narthecium, Odontostomum, Scoliopus, Stenanthium,*

Streptopus, Tofieldia, and *Xerophyllum*) are represented in California by a single species. An additional seven genera (*Bloomeria, Camassia, Clintonia, Disporum, Hastingsia, Smilacina,* and *Smilax*) are represented by only two species. Thus nearly one-half of all genera of Californian Liliaceae are represented by at best two taxa. The vast majority of these (eleven of the eighteen total) represent relictual taxa—i.e., geographically restricted species that formerly were more widespread.

However, the most characteristic genera of the California Liliaceae, arguably *Allium, Brodiaea,* and *Calochortus,* are comparatively species-rich taxa and thus may be considered as unusual representatives of the family in the state. This pattern holds true for the rare liliaceous species and infraspecific taxa in California—i.e., a few lily genera support most of the rare species for the family. For example, of the 101 lily taxa listed as rare in the *Inventory of Rare and Endangered Vascular Plants of California* (Skinner and Pavlik 1994), twenty-five belong to the genus *Calochortus,* seventeen to the genus *Allium,* thirteen to the genus *Fritillaria,* and twelve to the genus *Lilium.* Thus, the rare species within these four genera represent 67% of all lilies considered rare in California (Appendix B).

Lilium, Fritillaria, Erythronium, and *Calochortus* are the lily genera with the greatest proportion of their taxa endangered, threatened, rare, or uncommon (Appendix C). For example, 67% of all California's *Lilium* taxa are rare or uncommon. This is also true for 65% of the *Fritillaria* taxa, 62% of the *Erythronium* taxa, and 49% of the *Calochortus* taxa. The remaining lily genera have only a few rare species each.

In summary, California has a rich lily flora, represented primarily by two patterns. The first is that there are many genera of lilies that have one or a few species distributed rather widely throughout the state. Several of these taxa represent weedy exotics (e.g., *Ipheion, Muscari*); only two of these genera, *Androstephium* and *Bloomeria,* hold rare members. The second pattern is that only a few genera harbor most of the rare lilies in California. The most conspicuous members are the onions, mariposa lilies, fawn lilies, and fritillarias. Background for these observed patterns follows as a brief discussion of each California lily genus. Emphasis is placed on native taxa and species-rich genera.

Agave

(A G A V E)

Three species of *Agave* are found in California, although the genus includes nearly 300 taxa distributed throughout the warmer regions of the tropical Americas. Members of the genus are distinctive in that they produce very large, succulent rosettes bearing very large, long-lived, spine-tipped leaves. Each rosette typically reproduces only once and then dies. Inflorescences are large (up to four meters tall), bearing many white, light yellow, or purplish or red-tinged flowers. Several taxa, such as *Agave deserti,* are quite variable and hard to delimit taxonomically.

The three California species include *A. deserti*, characteristic of desert washes throughout the southwest United States and Baja California; *A. shawii*, considered rare in California because it is very narrowly restricted to only a few coastal bluffs in San Diego County; and, *A. utahensis*, an uncommon species of shadescale scrub and Joshua tree woodlands of California, Nevada, Utah, and Arizona. Many members of the genus were, and continue to be, important food plants for indigenous cultures throughout the Americas. Agaves provided many economic items, including a vegetable, fermented beverage (*pulque*), soapy liquid from the leaves, needles from the end spines, fishing poles from the inflorescence, and many fibers for saddle-cloths, sacks, ropes, nets, and cords.

Allium

(O N I O N)

The genus *Allium* is very large, with nearly 500 species occurring world-wide. Many species are important culinary crops—e.g., chives (*A. schoenoprasum*), garlic (*A. sativum*), onion (*A. cepa*), leeks (*A. porrum*), and shallots (*A. ascalonicum*). Indeed, the word *Allium* is derived from the classical Latin word for garlic, a species originating in the Mediterranean region. Thus the genus *Allium* is known for its strong odor that emanates from all parts of the plant when crushed or bruised. Sixty-three species and infraspecific *Allium* taxa occur in California, seventeen of which are considered rare.

All onions are perennial herbs, characterized by a many-coated bulb. *Allium* leaves are sometimes both cylindrical and hollow, and other times flat and solid. Flowers are produced on a leaf-less stem that blooms in a terminal array of flowers appearing to arise from the end of the flower stalk. Many onions are also cultivated for their horticultural beauty as well as their culinary appeal. Because of their distinctive morphology, physiology, and evolutionary history, some authors segregate onions into their own family, the Alliaceae, which also includes the subfamily Brodiaeinae (e.g., *Brodiaea*).

(A L O E)

Aloe is a large genus (250 species worldwide) distributed about the warmer regions of Mediterranean Europe, Asia, and Africa. Individuals of the genus are perennial (sometimes tree-like) herbs bearing large, fleshy leaves with a clasping base and thorny margins. Flowers support two perianth whorls that occur in two differentiated sets of three (six unequal stamens) and the flowers are produced on axillary inflorescences. *Aloe saponaria* x *A. striata*, a sterile hybrid, is a nonnative member of California's Liliaceae found in the coastal sage scrub of southern California. A native to South Africa, it has spread vegetatively from its original introduction in La Jolla, San Diego County.

(A N D R O S T E P H I U M)

The genus *Androstephium* consists of only two species, both of which are restricted to the southwestern United States. The name *Androstephium* is derived from the Greek words *andros*, meaning "stamen," and *stephanos*, meaning "crown." This designation is in apparent reference to the united staminal filaments that give this flower part its crown-like appearance. *Androstephium* is similar in appearance to the *Brodiaea–Dichelostemma–Triteleia* complex, but differs from all others by its fused staminal filaments, and from both *Brodiaea* and *Dichelostemma* by its six (not three) fertile stamens.

A single species of *Androstephium*, *A. breviflorum*, is found only occasionally in California, although it ranges from extreme southeastern California to southern Nevada, northern Arizona, southern Utah, and western Colorado. Botanists suggest that further documentation of the species' distribution in California is needed to understand its ecology, evolutionary history, and rare status.

Asparagus
(ASPARAGUS)

Asparagus is a very large genus of more than 300 species distributed widely throughout the temperate regions of the world. Individuals of the genus are generally dioecious and produce an erect or climbing stem from a rhizome bearing fleshy tubers. Leaves are characteristically scale-like, and thus members of the genus *Asparagus* can readily be identified.

Two exotic species of asparagus are found in California, *Asparagus asparagoides*, and *A. officinalis* ssp. *officinalis*. The former species is native to southern Africa, and is occasionally found in disturbed places in the San Francisco Bay area and along the south coast. *Asparagus officinalis* ssp. *officinalis* is the cultivated asparagus, and naturalized populations can be found occasionally throughout the state where asparagus has been grown commercially.

Asphodelus
(ASPHODEL)

Asphodelus is represented in the California Liliaceae by a single exotic species, *A. fistulosus*, a noxious weed found primarily in the southern San Joaquin Valley, and Monterey and San Luis Obispo Counties. Individuals of the genus are either annuals or short-lived perennials with basal, spiral, and linear leaves. The white or pinkish flowers are small and borne in panicles or racemes. *Asphodelphus fistulosus* is a lily that bears a tuber-like base, hollow stems, more or less cylindrical leaves, and an open panicle of white or pinkish flowers. The genus originates from southern Europe, although cultivated species of this group escape and become weedy members of many local floras in the warmer regions of the world.

Bloomeria

(GOLDENSTAR)

Bloomeria is a lily genus named after H.G. Bloomer, an early San Francisco botanist and former curator of botany at the California Academy of Sciences. It is one of several closely related genera (*Allium–Muilla–Bloomeria*), but is distinguished from the onions and *Muilla* primarily by its cup-like appendages at the base of each anther filament. *Bloomeria* plants thus consist of a corm enveloped by a fibrous coat; several long, narrow leaves; and an umbel-like inflorescence producing ten to more than thirty yellow flowers.

The genus consists of only two relictual species, *Bloomeria crocea*, the Common goldenstar, and *B. humilis*, the Dwarf goldenstar. Both species range from central and southern California into northern Baja California, Mexico. Neither is considered rare in California.

Brodiaea

(BRODIAEA)

The genus *Brodiaea* is restricted to western North America, ranging geographically from Vancouver, British Columbia in the north, to northern Baja California in the south. As currently understood, *Brodiaea* consists of sixteen species and four infraspecific taxa. Earlier researchers, however, recognized a larger genus with three subgenera, *Brodiaea*, *Triteleia*, and *Dichelostemma*. These "subgenera" are now regarded as distinct genera.

Brodiaea plants consist of a corm that grows annually and produces two to fifteen adjacent offset cormlets in the axils of old leaf bases. These cormlets generally will not flower until they reach a minimal size. *Brodiaea* cormlets also typically produce fleshy contractile roots that disperse the cormlet laterally away from the parent plant. Contractile roots also occur in seedlings, serving to draw the seedling's growing point as much as ten centimeters below the soil surface. Once a cormlet matures to adult size, production of contractile roots ceases.

Flowering for most species of *Brodiaea* begins in January and is achieved by the production of a leafless stem bearing a cluster of blue, purple, red, or white flowers. The flowers consist of six perianth segments, the outer ones being narrower than the inner whorl. The lower portion of all perianth segments are fused into a tube, which often bears purple stripes. Sterile stamens, or staminodia, are found opposite the outer perianth whorl and are distinctive in each species. These modified stamens are either attached to, leaning inward, or distinct from the functional, fertile stamens. Flowers of *Brodiaea* are self-incompatible; frequent pollinators include bee flies (Bombylidae), skipper butterflies (Herperiinae), tumbling flower beetles (Mordellidae), and sweat bees (Halictidae).

Brodiaea californica is one of the most common members of the genus. It is found widely throughout the open grasslands, woodlands, and chaparral of the outer North Coast Ranges and the northern Sierra Nevada. Harvest brodiaea (*B. elegans*) is perhaps even more common throughout the North Coast Ranges and Sierra Nevada, and can be found extending into southwestern Oregon. Dwarf brodiaea (*B. minor*) is yet another common and characteristic wildflower of California, found throughout the grasslands of the Sierra Nevada foothills, eastern Sacramento Valley, and northeastern San Joaquin Valley.

Many species of the genus are rare, and these include, among others, the Indian Valley brodiaea (*B. coronaria* ssp. *rosea*), an endangered species of the interior North Coast Range grasslands; Orcutt's brodiaea (*B. orcuttii*), a rare species of vernal pools and vernally moist grasslands in southern Riverside and San Diego Counties; and Chinese Camp brodiaea (*B. pallida*), an extremely endangered lily known from a single population in Tuolumne County. Individuals of *Brodiaea pallida* can, however, be found in cultivation.

Calochortus

(M A R I P O S A   L I L Y ,   F A I R Y   L A N T E R N ,   G L O B E   L I L Y)

Calochortus is a genus of approximately seventy species and infraspecific taxa, ranging from California to Nebraska, and from British Columbia to Guatemala. The name is derived from the Greek *kalos*, meaning "beautiful," and *chortus*, for "grass," in apt reference to the grasslike foliage of some mariposa lilies. Approximately fifty-one taxa occur in California and twenty-five of these—approximately 50%—are considered rare, endangered, threatened, or in decline. Members of *Calochortus* have been considered to compose a "monotypic" family (i.e., a family of plants represented by only one genus), the Calochortaceae, because of the unique combinations of chromosome numbers, obsolete or extremely short style, capsule dehiscence pattern, and morphological and developmental characters (i.e., polygonum-type embryo sac development).

The genus *Calochortus* has long been appreciated horticulturally for its striking tulip-like flowers. Certain species within the genus bear simple, undistinguished flowers (e.g., *C. uniflorus*), while other possess flowers of considerable petal complexity (e.g., *C. argillosus*). Nectaries (i.e., petal "glands") typically are present, and are found in a wide variety of shapes, adorned with various elaborate hairs, and often bear a protective membrane. The genus is notoriously difficult in cultivation being rather susceptible to various rots. However, a few species, for example the White globe lily (*C. albus*), are commonly found in cultivation.

Camassia

(C A M A S)

The genus *Camassia* consists of approximately four species distributed throughout North America. Individuals of the genus are bulbous perennials that occur either as a solitary bulb or in clusters, and each produces long basal leaves. Only one species (*C. quamash*) is found in California, but it is represented by two subspecies. *Ca-*

massia quamash ssp. *breviflora* bears bright yellow anthers and small perianth segments that are densely arranged along the inflorescence axis. *Camassia quamash* ssp. *quamash* bears larger flowers with dull yellow to violet anthers within flowers that are arranged in an open inflorescence. Neither California taxon is considered rare.

Camassia was an important food plant for the Native American tribes of California, as indicated by the Latin binomial being derived from the Native America name, *camas* or *quamash*. Native Americans boiled or roasted the bulb, and the roots provided a molasses-like syrup. *Camassia* is easily grown from seed or bulb.

Chlorogalum
(SOAPROOT, AMOLE)

This genus is distinctively Californian. It is one of the state's most characteristic bulb-forming genera, being found in a wide variety of habitats throughout the state and producing an extremely fibrous bulb coat. Five species have been consistently recognized since the original 1940 monographic treatment by the California botanist Robert F. Hoover, although several varieties of the five species are also currently recognized. Two of the five *Chlorogalum* species extend beyond California's borders: *Chlorogalum parviflorum* is found in Baja California (Mexico), and *C. pomeridianum*, stretches northward into the state of Oregon.

A constellation of lily genera of close evolutionary affinities includes *Camassia, Chlorogalum, Hesperocallis, Odontostomum,* and *Schoenolirion.* Soaproot likely is most closely related to *Camassia* and *Schoenolirion,* with all three genera bearing similar inflorescence structures and number of seeds. However, *Chlorogalum* can be easily distinguished from *Schoenolirion* by its smooth perianth that twists together over the ovary. *Chlorogalum* is distinguished from *Camassia* by the presence of fewer seeds in each locule, and by its inflorescence structure.

Rare *Chlorogalum* species in California include Red Hills soaproot (*C. grandiflorum*), dwarf soaproot (*C. pomeridianum* var. *minus*), Camatta Canyon amole (*C. purpureum* var. *reductum*), and purple amole (*C. purpureum* var. *purpureum*). Red Hills soaproot is a very localized species restricted to serpentinite substrates supporting open oak woodland and chaparral south of Chinese Camp. Camatta Canyon amole also is very localized, as it is known from a single occurrence near La Panza in the Los Padres National Forest. Dwarf soaproot is a variety of the common soaproot restricted to serpentine outcrops in the chaparral of the North and South Coast Ranges, and the purple amole is a rare species restricted to the eastern slope of the Santa Lucia Mountains in Monterey and San Luis Obispo Counties. Purple amole currently is under cultivation, which is fortunate because its dry woodland habitat is threatened by trampling, grazing, and off-road vehicular traffic.

Clintonia
(CLINTONIA)

The genus *Clintonia* was named for De Witt Clinton, a famous naturalist and early nineteenth century governor of New York. Although approximately six species represent the genus in North America as well as Asia, only two species, *Clintonia andrewsiana* and *C. uniflora*, are found in California. *Clintonia andrewsiana*, a perennial lily producing a slender rhizome, grows in redwood forests along the northern coastal regions of California (i.e., Klamath Plateau, North Coast region, and San Francisco Bay area), and it extends into southwestern Oregon. *Clintonia uniflora* also is distributed throughout the northern coastal regions, but unlike *C. andrewsiana*, extends eastward into the Sierra Nevada. The two California taxa differ primarily by their inflorescence structure. *Clintonia andrewsiana* bears pink to rose-colored flowers arranged in an umbel, while *C. uniflora* bears solitary white flowers. In California, the berries of *Clintonia* are a vivid blue. The genus is not commonly found in cultivation.

Dichelostemma
(DICHELOSTEMMA)

The genus *Dichelostemma* once was included as a distinct taxonomic section of the genus *Brodiaea*. Indeed, the genus appears very similar to *Brodiaea,* but is differentiated by an inflorescence stem that is generally curved or twisted (not straight), an umbel that is typically dense and not open, and staminal filaments that are crown-like, forming a tube outside the anthers. *Dichelostemma* is now recognized as a separate genus with five species and two additional infragenera taxa distributed throughout the western United States, but concentrated in northern California. The name, like many other California lilies, is descriptive of the flower morphology of a representative Californian species. It is derived from the Greek words *dichelos* for "bifid," and *stemma,* for "crown," referring to the bifid staminodes of *D. congestum*. Other California taxa include *Dichelostemma ida-maia, D. volubile, D. capitatum* ssp. *capitatum, D. capitatum* ssp. *pauciflorum,* and *D. multiflorum,* none of which are currently considered rare.

Disporum
(DISPORUM)

A genus of approximately fifteen species in temperate North America and eastern Asia, *Disporum* is characteristic of shady woodlands and forests throughout its range, including northern California. The name is derived from the Greek words meaning "double seed," in reference to its two-seeded fruits. Members of the genus produce slender, creeping rhizomes with erect, branching stems bearing alternate, sessile, or clasping leaves. The terminal inflorescences are typically umbel-like, and bear one to several whitish or greenish flowers that often are hidden by the leaves. *Disporum* is often identified by its yellow to red berries.

Two species are found in California. *Disporum hookeri* is restricted to northern California and the Sierra Nevada, extending into Montana and western Canada. *Disporum smithii* is restricted to the northwesternmost portion of California, extending from San Francisco Bay in the south to British Columbia in the north. Neither species is considered rare in California.

Erythronium

(FAWN LILY, DOG-TOOTHED VIOLET,
TROUT LILY)

Erythronium is a north temperate genus consisting of approximately twenty-five species, fourteen of which are found in California. Evolutionary relationships among the various species are poorly understood, although two informal groups of species may be distinguished in the western United States based on the presence or absence of mottled leaves. Individuals are bulbous perennials, although the bulb is somewhat elongate and bears one fleshy scale and bead-like segments of a rhizome. Only two basal leaves are produced in flowering plants, while non-reproductive individuals produce only one. One to ten nodding flowers are found on a leafless inflorescence; the perianth is large and showy, typically white, yellow, or white with a yellow base.

Little is known about the life history of California fawn lilies, despite their beauty and ability to grow in a variety of habitats. Only two rare species of *Erythronium* are illustrated within, but six additional rare *Erythronium* species are found in California. Henderson's fawn lily (*Erythronium hendersonii*), for example, is considered rare in the state, being restricted to dry woodlands on the Klamath Plateau of northern California and adjacent Oregon. Interestingly, Henderson's fawn lily is known to hybridize freely with the lemon-colored fawn lily (*E. citrinum* var. *citrinum*) in Oregon; it differs from the lemon-colored fawn lily by its mottled leaves, purple perianth, and pale brown or purple anthers. Howell's fawn lily (*Erythronium howellii*), Klamath fawn lily (*Erythronium klamathense*), Shuteye Peak fawn lily (*Erythronium pluriflorum*), and Hocket Lakes fawn lily (*Erythronium pusaterii*) are considered rare in California. Most of these, as well as the common members, are difficult to cultivate.

Fritillaria

(FRITILLARY, ADOBE LILY)

Fritillaria is a lily genus of approximately eighty taxa distributed widely in the Northern Hemisphere. The name derives from the Latin word *fritillus* for "dice box," in reference to the shape of the capsule, which is squarish and "rattles" when dry. Individuals are produced from a bulb typically with one or a few large fleshy scales and often several smaller ones. Leaves either alternate or form a whorl, and support a several-flowered inflorescence. All six perianth segments are similar in appearance, and a nectary is found on each. *Fritillaria* flowers are nodding and bell-shaped, and many are a distinctive purple-brown.

The genus consists of approximately twenty species in California, where most are rather uniform in shape and color, and comprised of few infraspecific taxa. This is in striking contrast to the mariposa lilies. However, like *Calochortus*, many *Fritillaria* bulbs were eaten by Native Americans, and many California *Fritillaria* species are quite difficult to cultivate. Some Old World taxa, e.g., the 'crown Imperial' Fritillary (*F. imperialis*), have long been in cultivation. As with many of the California lilies, very little is known about the ecology and evolution of this distinctive genus in North America.

Rare *Fritillaria* species in California include stinkbells (*Fritillaria agrestis*), Ojai fritillary (*Fritillaria ojaiensis*), adobe lily (*Fritillaria pluriflora*), Purdy's fritillary (*Fritillaria purdyi*), Roderick's fritillary (*Fritillaria roderickii*), Striped adobe lily (*Fritillaria striata*), Marin checker lily (*Fritillaria affinis* var. *tristulis*), Hillsborough chocolate lily (*Fritillaria biflora* var. *ineziana*), Greenhorn fritillary (*Fritillaria brandegei*), Butte County fritillary (*Fritillaria eastwoodiae*), talus fritillary (*Fritillaria falcata*), fragrant fritillary (*Fritillaria liliacea*), and San Benito fritillary (*Fritillaria viridea*). Many of these rare taxa are known from one or a few populations (e.g., *F. ojaiensis*, *F. roderickii*). The Marin checker lily is known from less than ten populations, some of which are threatened by grazing. Interestingly the plants of *F. affinis* var. *tristulis* appear to reproduce only by bulblets, because the fruits apparently do not contain viable seed.

Some rare species are threatened by horticultural collecting (e.g., *F. pluriflora*). The Hillsborough chocolate lily, however, is found on serpentinite soils of the southern portion of the San Francisco Bay area, and is not as threatened with extinction as are other *Fritillaria* species. The Greenhorn fritillary is threatened by logging, and because it grows in the openings in the coniferous forests of the southern Sierra Nevada of Kern and Tulare Counties, it is also threatened by deer and cattle grazing. The Butte County fritillary is threatened with land development and logging on private lands. It, like the talus fritillary, fragrant fritillary, and San Benito fritillary, is found on serpentinite talus slopes of central and northern California.

Hastingsia

(HASTINGSIA)

The genus *Hastingsia* represents a segregate genus from *Schoenolirion*, a lily genus characteristic of the southeastern United States. Thus California species of *Hastingsia* were formerly assigned to the genus *Schoenolirion*. Individuals are bulbous perennials with basal, grass-like leaves and an inflorescence of twenty to approximately seventy small white, yellowish, or greenish flowers. Of the four species known, two are found in California, although neither is considered rare. *Hastingsia alba* typically is found in wet meadows and bogs of northern California and adjacent Oregon. *Hastingsia serpentinicola* is found in the drier habitats underlain by well-drained serpentinite, also in northwestern California and southwestern Oregon.

Hesperocallis

(DESERT LILY)

The monotypic desert or ajo lily (*Hesperocallis undulata*), is a relictual species found in sandy or gravelly soils of the Mojave and Sonoran deserts of California, Arizona, northern Sonora and northern and central Baja California (Mexico). The name is derived from the Greek, *hesperos*, meaning "evening," and *kallos*, meaning "beauty." Individuals of *H. undulata* are deeply buried bulbous perennials that bear long, rather narrow, wavy, blue-green leaves with white margins. Eight or more fragrant flowers are produced on a single infloresence, and each bears white tepals with a green midstripe.

Bulbs of the desert lily once provided a staple food for the Native Americans of the southwestern U.S. Although difficult to grow

in cultivation and consequently uncommon in gardens, it was introduced into the horticultural arena in 1882. Presently this monotypic
genus is not considered rare in California.

Ipheion

(STAR FLOWER)

Ipheion uniflorum is an exotic species native to Argentina. Its taxonomy has long been confused, as the species has been placed by
some botanists in various other genera, e.g., *Muilla*, *Triteleia*, and
Brodiaea. Some still consider star flower to be *Brodiaea uniflora*, for
example. Like many other lilies, it is a delicate ornamental of under-
stated beauty, and has been in cultivation for more than 150 years. Its
flowers are fragrant, but the broken or crushed foliage bears a garlic
odor. Star flower can found in disturbed places in urban areas throughout the warmer portions of the state.

Leucrocrinum

(SAND LILY)

Like the desert lily (*Hesperocallis undulata*), sand lily (*Leucro-
crinum montanum*) is a relictual monotypic taxon widely distributed
in the western United States. The name *Leucocrinum* is Greek for
"white lily." *Leucocrinum montanum* is a perennial that rises from a
deep caudex and fleshy roots. The basal leaves are long and linear;
flowers arise from an underground pedicel. The large perianth is partly
fused and a showy white. Like the flower pedicels, the superior ovary
is borne underground and matures into a three-angled capsule. In
California, this distinctive lily can be found in sandy flats, sagebrush
scrub, and montane forests of the Klamath Region and eastward across
the Modoc Plateau.

Lilium

(LILY)

The genus *Lilium* is represented by approximately one hundred species distributed circumboreally. The name is an old Latin name similar to the Greek *leirion*, used by Theophrastus in reference to the Madonna lily (*Lilium candidum*). Approximately twenty-one species of *Lilium* are found in North America, of which eighteen taxa grow in California. Eleven of these eighteen are considered rare, threatened, endangered, or uncommon in the state. Most of the western North American species and twelve of the Californian taxa are of the turk's cap (*Martagon*) morphology—i.e., large species with spotted, orange or yellow pendant flowers with strongly reflexed tepals and exserted stamens. Other species possess a tubular perianth of various sizes and orientation.

Rare *Lilium* species in California include the Bolander's lily (*L. bolanderi*), Humboldt lily (*L. humboldtii*), ocellated Humbolt lily (*L. humboldtii* ssp. *ocellatum*), coast lily (*L. maritimum*), western lily (*L. occidentale*), Pitkin Marsh lily (*L. pitkinense*), Vollmer's lily (*L. vollmeri*), Kellogg's lily (*L. kelloggii*), lemon lily (*L. parryi*), redwood lily (*L. rubescens*), and purple-flowered Washington lily (*L. purpurascens*).[1] Virtually all of these lily species are known from only a few populations and are threatened primarily by horticultural collection and urban development. The lemon lily, for example, has nearly been extirpated in San Diego County, although a few plants still may remain on Palomar Mountain. In addition to collection and development, this rare species is also threatened by water diversions and livestock grazing.

Maianthemum

(F A L S E   L I L Y - O F - T H E - V A L L E Y)

Maianthemum is a small north temperate genus consisting of only three species, one of which, *Maianthemum dilatatum*, is found in California. The name is derived from the Greek words *maios*, for "May,"

---

[1] *The Jepson Manual* (Hickman 1993) includes the Pitkin Marsh lily as *L. pardalinum* ssp. *pitkinense*), Vollmer's lily as *L. pardalinum* ssp. *vollmeri*, and the Purple-flowered Washington lily *L. washingtonianum* ssp. *purpurescens*, based upon the doctoral work of Dr. Mark Skinner (see Chapter 3). However, these subspecific names have not been validly published, and should not be recognized.

and *anthemon*, for "blossom," to refer to its time of flowering. False lily-of-the-valley is a very wide-ranging species, stretching from Alaska southward to the northern portion of the state, and eastward into Idaho. It is typically found in large populations growing in the moist shade of north temperate coniferous forests. Twenty or more flowers are borne on zig-zag stems, and are subtended by two, often heart-shaped leaves. It is also an unusual lily in that the flowers bear only four tepals and four stamens.

(M U I L L A)

The genus *Muilla* consists of approximately six species distributed throughout California, Nevada, and Baja California (Mexico). The name *Muilla* is an anagram of *Allium*, proposed because of its superficial resemblance to the onion genus. Some botanists place this genus in the segregate family Alliaceae, while others place it in the Amaryllidaceae. However, *Muilla* likely is most closely related to the *Brodiaea–Triteleia–Dichelostemma* complex of genera, as it is a genus of cormous perennials with more or less cylindrical leaves and an umbel-like inflorescence of three to thirty flowers.

Four species, *Muilla clevelandii*, *M. coronata*, *M. maritima*, and *M. transmontana*, are found in the state; two species are considered rare. The rare San Diego goldenstar (*M. clevelandii*) is a cormous perennial of the mesa grasslands and coastal scrub edges within southwest San Diego County. Crowned muilla (*M. coronata*) is somewhat more widespread, found across the eastern slope of the southern Sierra Neveda, Mojave Desert, and western Nevada. It is characteristic of the open desert scrub and piñon woodland of these regions.

(G R A P E   H Y A C I N T H)

Grape hyacinth (*Muscari botryoides*) is a weedy member of the moderately large genus *Muscari*. It is characteristic of much of the temperate Old World, having long been in cultivation. Its name derives from the Greek word *moschos*, for "musk," in reference to the scent of some species. Individuals of grape hyacinth arise from rather small, round bulbs which produce few grass-like leaves and a dense inflorescence of small, bluish, bell-shaped flowers. Like the star flower (*Ipheion*), grape hyacinth typically is found in disturbed urban areas, such as abandoned gardens and abandoned lots in addition to cultivated settings.

Narthecium
(B O G   A S P H O D E L)

The Bog asphodel belongs to a lily genus consisting of four species, only one of which is found in California. *Narthecium californicum* is a relictual taxon characterized by a rhizomatous stem with densely overlapping, grass-like basal leaves and a tall inflorescence of small, yellow-green flowers. California's *Narthecium californicum* is not counted among the rare lilies, being found commonly in wet meadows and along streams in the Klamath Region and North Coast Ranges, as well as in the Sierra Nevada.

Nolina
(B E A R G R A S S)

The genus *Nolina* consists of approximately twenty-five species that are primarily restricted to the deserts of southwestern United States and adjacent Mexico. Four taxa of *Nolina* are found in California—*N. interrata*, *N. bigelovii*, *N. parryi*, and *N. cismontana*. *Nolina interrata* is considered endangered in California.

Individuals of *Nolina* are typically tree-like, polycarpic shrubs bearing unisexual flowers on tall inflorescences. Male and female flowers are found on separate individuals, such that species of *Nolina* are considered "dioecious,"—of two "houses." Interestingly, the functionally staminate flowers produce abortive pistils, and the pistillate flowers produce sterile anthers, leading some to conclude (incorrectly) that the flowers are bisexual. Sword-like leaves are clustered in dense rosettes. Members of the genus superficially resemble those of *Agave*, but instead, are distinguished from *Agave* primarily by position of the ovary. In *Nolina* the ovary is superior, while it is inferior in the genus *Agave*. The genus, however, is one of four (*Nolina, Dasylirion, Beaucarnea,* and *Calibanus*) that form a natural group of southern United States and Central American xerophytic monocots. *Nolina* and *Dasylirion* are found in both the United States and Central America, while the remaining taxa, *Beaucarnea* and *Calibanus*, are not distributed north of the Mexican border. The center of diversity for the genus *Nolina* is probably the tablelands of temperate Mexico; it is undoubtedly of an ancient origin.

Nothoscordum

(FALSE GARLIC)

False garlic (*Nothoscordum gracile*) is considered a noxious weed in California and is commonly found in disturbed areas throughout the state. Estimates on the number of species in this American genus vary widely, from three to thirty-five, but only one is found in California. Its name is derived from the Greek words *nothos*, for "false," and *skorodon*, for "garlic." Similar to *Allium*, it differs from true onions primarily because it does not bear any onion odor, as evidenced by its scientific name. False garlic is characterized by a bulb with basal bulblets, flat or channeled basal leaves, and an umbel-like inflorescence. The perianth is a distinctive white with greenish bases and red midveins. Virtually all species in cultivation have the potential to escape from their garden settings.

Odontostomum

(ODONTOSTOMUM)

The genus *Odontostomum* is known by a single species, *O. hartwegii*. It is named from the Greek words, *odon*, for "tooth" and *stoma*, for "mouth," apparently in reference to the six distinctive staminodia. Individual plants arise from a corm and support linear basal leaves and a paniculate inflorescence. Perianth segments are partly fused below, with the perianth lobes spreading or reflexed. Six stamens are attached to the perianth and alternate with the six staminodia. The anthers are rather unusual for the California lilies in that they dehisce pollen through pores at the tip. *Odontostomum hartwegii* is not rare in California. It is a relictual species often found within the inner North Coast Ranges and foothills of the Sierra Nevada on clay soils typically derived from serpentinite.

Scoliopus

(F E T I D   A D D E R ' S   T O N G U E)

Two species of *Scoliopus* are found along the western coast of the United States, one of which grows in California. The name *Scoliopus* derives from a Greek word meaning "crooked foot," a reference to the plant's curved pedicels. Other distinctive morphological features of Fetid adder's tongue include a short, slender rhizome; two sheathing, mottled basal leaves; and an umbel-like inflorescence with slightly malodorous greenish or yellowish flowers that are distinctly purple or dark-brown veined. *Scoliopus bigelovii*, like many other relictual lilies, is typically found in moist, shady redwood forests and adjacent chaparral in the outer North Coast Ranges and in the San Francisco Bay area.

Smilacina

(F A L S E   S O L O M O N ' S   S E A L)

Approximately twenty-five species of *Smilacina* are found in the north temperate regions of the world. The name *Smilacina* derives from the Greek meaning "little smilax," as this genus superficially resembles another lily genus, *Smilax*. *Smilacina* is a rhizomatous perennial with an erect stem bearing alternate leaves. The terminal inflorescence supports as many as twenty or more white flowers that when pollinated, mature into red or purplish berries.

Two species of *Smilacina* are found in California, although neither one is considered rare. Both *Smilacina racemosa* and *S. stellata* are found on moist streambanks and woodlands throughout the state. They differ in that the latter species, *S. stellata*, supports an inflorescence that is a raceme bearing larger flowers than *S. racemosa*. The former species produces a paniculate inflorescence.

Smilax

(C A T   C L A W ,   G R E E N B R I A R)

Smilax is a large liliaceous genus of approximately 350 species distributed worldwide. Many species of *Smilax*, for example, are conspicuous vines in tropical or semitropical moist forests. They are a distinctive group of lilies in that they are dioecious perennials arising from a tuber-like caudex with a climbing or trailing stem. The leaves are simple, alternate, and have rounded or arrow-shaped bases. The inflorescence is typically a many-flowered, axillary cluster of white, greenish, or yellowish flowers that when pollinated mature into berries of various colors.

Only two species of *Smilax* are found in California. *Smilax californica* is a riparian vine found along streambanks in the coniferous forests in the northern portion of the state. English Peak greenbriar (*Smilax jamesii*) is considered a rare species in California, occasionally found along lakes, streambanks, and in alder groves within montane coniferous forests of the Klamath region.

Stenanthium

(S T E N A N T H I U M)

Stenanthium occidentale is the only California member of this lily genus that consists of five species. The name *Stenanthium* derives from the Greek phrase for "narrow flower," in obvious reference to its partly fused tepals and narrow, bell-shaped corolla. Other distinguishing characteristics of members of the genus *Stenanthium* include the presence of a bulb; mostly basal, grass-like leaves; an inflorescence of nodding, sometimes unisexual flowers with a partly fused perianth; and a partly inferior ovary. The five species are found throughout western North America and Mexico. *Stenanthium occidentale*, as well as other members of the genus, is a relictual species charactistically found in moist meadows, thickets, and streambanks in the Klamath Plateau and throughout northwestern United States and Canada.

(T W I S T E D - S T A L K)

Seven species of *Streptopus* are distributed throughout North America and Eurasia; most of the taxa are wide-ranging. Individuals of the genus are identified by their long, horizontal rhizomes, alternate leaves, and one- to two-flowered axillary inflorescences of bell- or saucer-shaped flowers that mature into greenish or dark red berries. As with *Stenanthium*, only one taxon of this small lily genus is found in California. *Streptopus amplexifolius* var. *americanus* typically can be found in moist, shaded environments in the northern portion of the state, extending northward to Alaska and eastward into the central portion of the continent.

(T O F I E L D I A)

Tofieldia is a genus of approximately fifteen species, named after the eighteenth century British botanist, Thomas Tofield. Only a single species, *Tofieldia occidentalis* ssp. *occidentalis*, is found in California. It is a rhizomatous lily with an erect stem, both grass-like basal leaves and sheathing cauline leaves on the lower portion of the stem, and a short, terminal inflorescence. Flowers are white, greenish, or yellowish, and bear a superior ovary with three-lobes at the tip. Like many of the other common and relictual lilies of California, it is a taxon characteristic of moist habitats (e.g., fens, wet meadows) in the northern portion of the state and elsewhere.

(W A K E R O B I N ,   W O O D   L I L Y)

Trillium is a genus of perennial herbs characteristic of temperate forests in three disjunct geographic regions: eastern Asia, eastern North America, and western North America. The name *Trillium* is derived from the Latin word *tris*, in reference to the three stem leaves and three-parted flower. This lily genus presents considerable taxonomic challenges because of the great variety of individual forms found within and among populations. Of the thirty to forty described species, only five are found in California.

Species of *Trillium* are easily distinguished by the three leaves that are borne in an apical whorl, and the solitary flower that is either stalked or sessile. The outer perianth whorl is often leaf-like, and the inner, petaloid whorl ranges in color from green-yellow to white, to pink or dark maroon. The leaves are also distinctive, as they are typically glossy and soft, and often mottled silver-white or purple. All *Trillium* species are found in rich moist woods or shrub-lands.

Two of the five Californian species are considered rare. Western trillium (*Trillium ovatum*) has the infraspecific taxon, Salmon Mountains wakerobin (*Trillium ovatum* ssp. *oettingeri*), which is protected by the U.S. Forest Service in the Marble Mountains of Siskiyou County. The other rare *Trillium* species in California, brook wakerobin (*Trillium rivale*), grows along rocky streambanks in the Klamath region and in adjacent Oregon.

Triteleia

(TRITELEIA)

Triteleia is a genus of approximately fourteen species, restricted to the western portion of North America. Thirteen species (seventeen taxa) are found in California. The name *Triteleia* is derived from the Greek *trios*, "three," and *teleios*, "complete," referring to the flower parts that are consistently found in threes. Species of *Triteleia* are characterized by a fibrous-coated corm that bears one to two narrow basal leaves and an inflorescence of many blue, white, or lilac-colored flowers. *Triteleia* is similar to the genus *Brodiaea*, but is distinguished from the latter primarily by its six fertile stamens and the absence of staminodia. *Triteleia* is found in a variety of habitats, including rocky cliffs, open conifer forests, sage grasslands, and vernally wet meadows.

Five taxa are considered rare in California. These include yellow triteleia (*Triteleia crocea* var. *crocea*), Trinity Mountains triteleia (*T. crocea* var. *modesta*), San Clemente Island triteleia (*T. clementina*), Henderson's triteleia (*T. hendersonii* var. *hendersonii)*, and Cook's triteleia (*T. ixioides* ssp. *cookii*). Most rare species of *Triteleia* are not as restricted or threatened as other lily taxa. However, the San Clemente Island triteleia grows on the damp rock walls on the Channel Island of San Clemente, and is quite rare, being known from less than twenty occurrences.

Veratrum

(F A L S E   H E L L E B O R E)

Like many other liliaceous genera, *Veratrum* is a complex genus of approximately thirty species of rather coarse perennials distributed throughout the Northern Hemisphere. Its name is derived from the Latin *vere*, meaning "true," and *ater*, meaning "black." This is in reference to the black (and highly toxic) rhizome of many of the species.

Individuals of *Veratrum* produce erect, stout, and leafy stems with a terminal inflorescence of rather small but numerous flowers. The flowers can be either white, purple, red-brown, or greenish white and mature into capsules. The genus is characteristic of montane wet meadows and open woodlands.

Four species of *Veratrum* occur in California, two of which are considered rare. The Siskiyou false hellebore (*Veratrum insolitum*) ranges from northern California to Oregon and Washington, but it is a lily rarely encountered in its habitat of openings in thickets and mixed-evergreen forests. *Veratrum insolitum* is distinguished by its densely hairy ovary and its irregularly to shallowly fringed petals. The uncommon fringed false hellebore (*Veratrum fimbriatum*) is found in wet meadows amongst the coastal scrub of Mendocino and Sonoma Counties within the North Coast Ranges.

Individuals of the genus possess many alkaloids, some of which have been used medicinally. Many, however, are toxic to humans and livestock.

Xerophyllum

(BEAR-GRASS, INDIAN BASKET-GRASS)

Bear-grass is a distinctive lily genus consisting of two species in North America, only one of which, the relictual *Xerophyllum tenax*, is found in California. Individuals arise from a woody, tuber-like rhizome that persists many years before flowering. The simple stem is stout and supports many persistent, wiry, grass-like leaves. The inflorescence of bear-grass is a dense, club-shaped cluster of up to one hundred small, whitish or cream-colored flowers. *Xenophyllum tenax* is a common Bear-grass distributed along dry open slopes, ridges, and in coniferous forests in many portions of the state. It is not considered rare in California.

Yucca

(SPANISH BAYONET)

Yucca is a lily genus of approximately forty species characteristic of the dry regions of North America. Individuals are somewhat tree-like, with rosetted leaves either basal or elevated on branches. The inflorescence of the *Yucca* is a large, dense panicle of erect, spreading, or pendant, fleshy, white flowers. The *Yucca* genus is well known for the noctural pollination of its flowers by "yucca moths" that simultaneously lay eggs in the flower ovary.

Several taxa, e.g., *Yucca brevifolia*, define distinctive communities (i.e., Joshua tree woodlands) of the American southwest. Others, such as *Y. whipplei*, have generated distinctive common names (Our Lord's candle), in this instance because of the species' extremely tall inflorescence. Four species (*Yucca baccata*, *Y. brevifolia*, *Y. schidigera*, and *Y. whipplei*) are found in California and none are considered rare or uncommon.

Zigadenus

(DEATH CAMAS)

Zigadenus is a genus of approximately fifteen species distributed in temperate North America and in Asia. The name is derived from the Greek *zygon*, for "yoke," and *aden*, for "gland," as the perianth glands are sometimes found in pairs at the tepal base. Individuals arise from a bulb or rhizome and produce an array of long basal leaves. The inflorescence in most species bears perfect yellowish- or greenish-white flowers on a panicle or raceme. *Zigadenus paniculatus*, however, bears bisexual, staminate, and sometimes sterile flowers on the same inflorescence.

Seven taxa are found within California, and many are characteristic of meadows, woodlands, and sagebrush scrub slopes of the foothill regions. No rare species of *Zigadenus* are found in California. All taxa are highly toxic to livestock and to humans as well, as they contain steroidal alkaloids that cause vomiting, respiratory difficulties, and a coma if eaten.

FIGURE 1

Fig. 1.1. Selected morphological characteristics of the California Liliaceae (not to scale). Underground stem: (A) corm (Muilla); (B) bulb with fibrous bulb coat (Chlorogalum); (C) caudex (Leucocrinum). Above ground stem: (D) erect, simple, herbaceous stem (Hesperocallis).

Fig. 1.2. (E) branching, tree-like stem (Yucca); (F) vining stem (Smilax). Leaves: (G) alternating stem leaves (Smilacina); (H) whorled stem leaves (Lilium).

Fig. 1.3. (I) whorled grass-like basal leaves (Narthecium). Perianth: (J) 6 similar tepals in 2 whorls of three (Zigadenus); (K) 6 tepals in 2 different whorls of three—the outer "sepals" and the inner "petals" (Calochortus). Androecium: (L) 6 fertile stamens with simple filaments (Hastingsia).

Fig. 1.4. (M) fertile stamens and infertile staminodia (Brodiaea); (N) 3 fertile stamens with filaments fused to perianth in a crown-like tube (Triteleia). Gynoecium: (O) superior ovary with 3 stigmas (Tofieldia); (P) superior ovary with prominent crests and three-lobed stigma (Allium).

Fig. 1.5. Fruit: (Q) capsule (Camassia); (R) berry (Maianthemum).

Illustrations are reprinted with permission from the University of California Press and the University of California Jepson Herbarium.

(A)

(B)

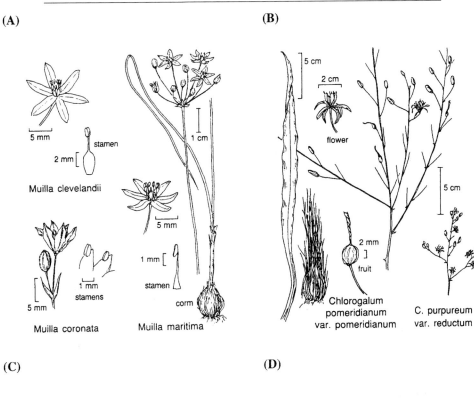

5 mm

stamen

2 mm

Muilla clevelandii

1 cm

5 mm

Muilla coronata

1 mm

stamens

5 mm

1 mm

stamen

corm

Muilla maritima

5 cm

2 cm

flower

5 cm

2 mm

fruit

Chlorogalum
pomeridianum
var. pomeridianum

C. purpureum
var. reductum

(C)

(D)

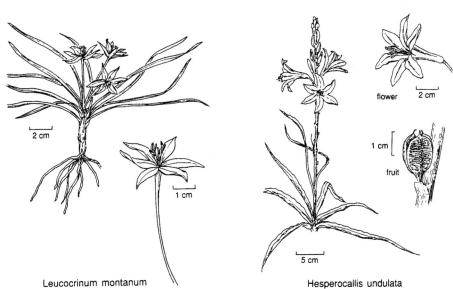

2 cm

1 cm

Leucocrinum montanum

flower   2 cm

1 cm

fruit

5 cm

Hesperocallis undulata

FIGURE 1.1

(E)

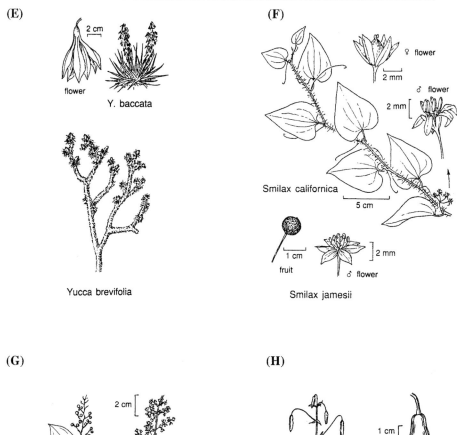

2 cm

flower

Y. baccata

Yucca brevifolia

(F)

♀ flower

2 mm

♂ flower

2 mm

Smilax californica

5 cm

fruit

1 cm

2 mm

♂ flower

Smilax jamesii

(G)

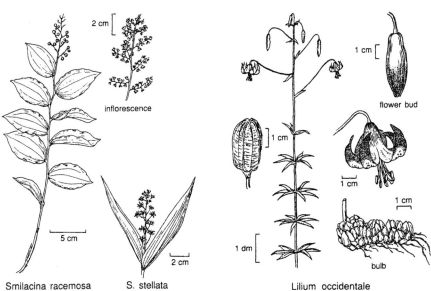

2 cm

inflorescence

5 cm

2 cm

Smilacina racemosa   S. stellata

(H)

1 cm

flower bud

1 cm

1 cm

1 cm

1 dm

bulb

Lilium occidentale

FIGURE 1.2

(I)

(J)

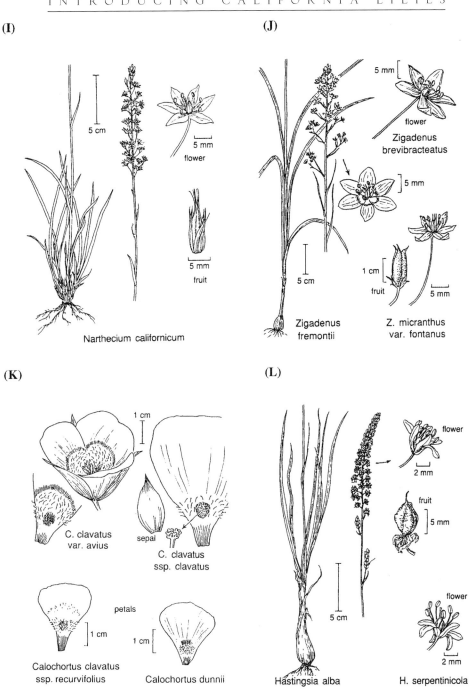

Narthecium californicum

Zigadenus brevibracteatus

flower

Zigadenus fremontii

Z. micranthus var. fontanus

(K)

C. clavatus var. avius

sepal

C. clavatus ssp. clavatus

petals

Calochortus clavatus ssp. recurvifolius

Calochortus dunnii

(L)

Hastingsia alba

flower

fruit

H. serpentinicola

flower

FIGURE 1.3

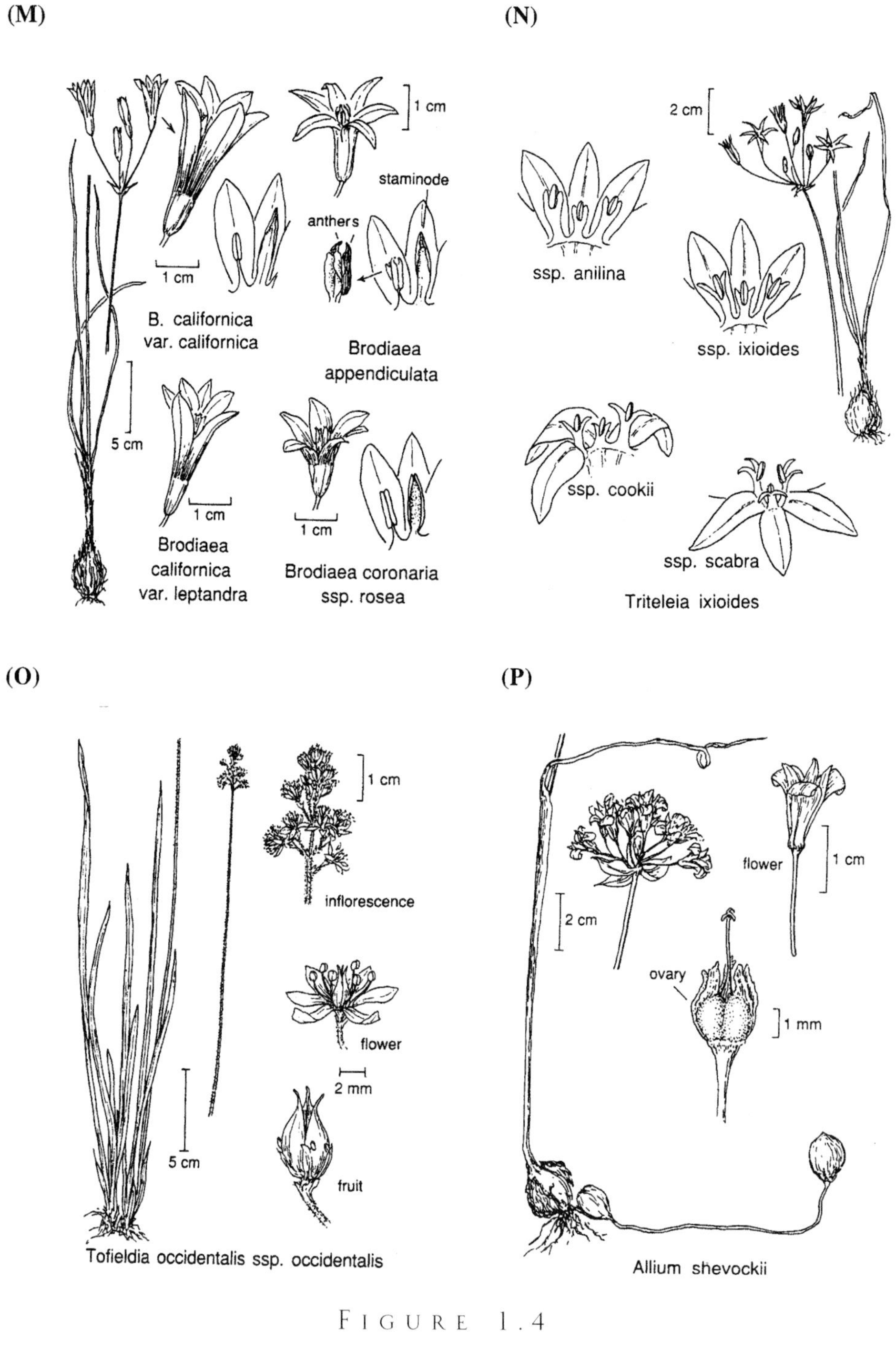

(M)

(N)

1 cm

staminode

anthers

B. californica
var. californica

Brodiaea
appendiculata

5 cm

1 cm

Brodiaea
californica
var. leptandra

1 cm

Brodiaea coronaria
ssp. rosea

2 cm

ssp. anilina

ssp. ixioides

ssp. cookii

ssp. scabra

Triteleia ixioides

(O)

(P)

1 cm

inflorescence

flower

2 mm

fruit

5 cm

Tofieldia occidentalis ssp. occidentalis

flower

1 cm

2 cm

ovary

1 mm

Allium shevockii

FIGURE 1.4

(Q)

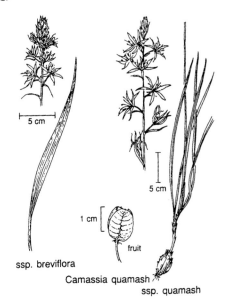

ssp. breviflora

Camassia quamash
ssp. quamash

(R)

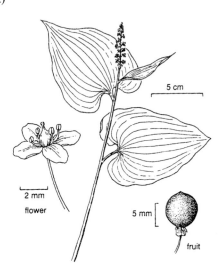

Maianthemum dilatatum

F I G U R E   1 . 5

Chapter 2

PATTERNS OF RARITY
IN CALIFORNIA'S
LILIES

L ilies can be rare for an astonishing variety of reasons. Sometimes
they are rare because their habitat is very limited or because the
habitat has been converted by humans to other uses. It is useful, therefore, to distinguish between two major types of rarity: natural rarities
and anthropogenic rarities. Natural rarities are those species that,
during their evolutionary history, have always been rare, or currently
are rare by today's standards. The word *endemic* is often used to describe natural rarities that are confined to a specific habitat or geographic area. Anthropogenic rarities are those species that were formerly more widespread, but through habitat alteration or other forms
of disturbance by humans, are either greatly fragmented or restricted
to a few small, imperiled populations. Each of these types of rarity
has its own set of consequences that must be considered for lily conservation and management.

PATTERNS OF RARITY
IN CALIFORNIA LILIACEAE

What does it mean to be rare? Using the word "rare" is really a
statement about the geographic distribution and abundance of a particular plant species. Therefore, rarity describes at least three very
different biological properties. A rare taxon can be (1) broadly distributed, but never abundant where found; (2) narrowly distributed
or clumped and abundant where found; or, (3) narrowly distributed
or clumped and not abundant where found. Geographic definitions
of rarity can also include a temporal component, such that a rare species is defined by its population size, distribution, and persistence
through geologic time.

An important and particularly persuasive classification of natural rarities ties a species' potential habitat restriction to its geographic distribution and its population size (Rabinowitz, 1981) (Appendix D). Seven possible forms of rarity have been identified, six of which can be used to classify rarities for various geographic regions. For example, the Tiburon mariposa lily (*Calochortus tiburonensis*) is found in great numbers only on an unusual soil ("serpentinite") on only one mountaintop of the Tiburon Penninsula in the San Francisco Bay area. Thus this species is a habitat "specialist," geographically restricted, but abundant where found. The Dehesa nolina (*Nolina interrata*) is found in gabbroic or serpentinite chaparral throughout San Diego County and Baja California, Mexico, but unlike the Tiburon mariposa lily, is never found in large numbers.

Another example is the Alkali mariposa (*Calochortus striatus*), a rare lily that predictably can be found around desert springs and in wet meadows throughout the Mojave Desert. Thus, it has a broad geographic distribution, narrow habitat requirements, and typically large population sizes. The crowned muilla (*Muilla coronata*) is widely distributed throughout southeastern California and Nevada, but never occurs as a dominant plant in the landscape. Therefore, this rare lily also has a wide geographic distribution and broad habitat requirements, but is never found as a large, locally dominant population.

One of the drawbacks of this classification scheme, however, is that a likely *cause* of rarity, such as a limited habitat, cannot be distinguished from a likely *consequence* of rarity, such as decreased resistence to disease. In practice it is often difficult to distinguish between cause and consequence, particularly because we know so little about the biology of rare organisms in general. However, the goal of conserving biological diversity will be better served if politicians, developers, and conservationists understand that there are different patterns of rarity among plants, and that those patterns may require different forms of protection and management.

C A U S E S   O F   R A R I T Y

A starting point in understanding causes of rarity can be found in Table 2. This generalized list of probable causes of rarity for natu-

---

T A B L E   2

Classes of probable causes of rarity in plant species

1. Age
2. Coevolution
3. Earth History
4. Ecology
5. Evolutionary History
6. Genetics
7. Life History "Strategies"
8. Population Dynamics
9. Reproductive Biology
10. Chance Events (Environmental and Demographic)
11. Taxonomic History
12. Human Uses
13. Land Use History

Adapted from Fiedler and Ahouse, 1992.

ral and anthropogenic rarities identifies thirteen broad categories of factors that contribute to rarity. The first ten causes are related to the biology of rare species, while the last three categories of causes are related to human activities. For example, the general category "Human Uses" includes the specific causes of horticultural trade, aboriginal uses, and exploitation by ancient and/or modern medicine. Many California lilies, including species of onion (*Allium*) and mariposa lilies (*Calochortus*), were eaten by the Native Americans, while other lilies, e.g., the genus *Lilium*, have been extremely important in the horticultural trade for over one hundred years. Almost all of the California *Lilium* species are threatened with population extinction by enthusiastic lily collectors.

The general category "Age" includes correlates of different ages—i.e., old age, youthfulness, and intermediate age (and therefore not likely to be relevant). In California, many plant species are rare because they are either new species, termed "neoendemics," or old species, termed "paleoendemics." New species are often found in geologically new or youthful habitats; thus rarity is partly a function of a new species' youth. As such, these species have not had time to significantly expand their geographic range from their point of origin to their climatic or edaphic limits. Such rarities include, for example, *Brodiaea pallida*, a rare lily that exists as a single population that is restricted to vernally moist, serpentinite streambeds in Tuolumne County. In contrast, some of California's most famous species, such as the Giant sequoia (*Sequoiadendron giganteum*) and Monterey pine (*Pinus radiata*), are old species formerly more broadly distributed geographically, but now have retreated to their current ranges in response to more recent climatic changes. Many California lilies fall into this category as presumed relictual species (e.g., *Tofieldia occidentalis* ssp. *occidentalis, Narthecium californicum, Hesperocallis undulata, Odontostomum hartwegii, Smilax californica, Stenanthium occidentale, Xerophyllum tenax, Scoliopus bigelovii, Hastingsia alba,* and *Bloomeria crocea*).

Another important classification of California rarities is based primarily on age, but also on genetic characteristics. It includes paleoendemics as well as "patroendemics," "schizoendemics," and "apoendemics"—the latter three categories are largely various forms of young species distinguished by their chromosome complement. Two categories in this classification system are especially important because they contain many of California's rare species. Patroendemics are often rare species with a normal chromosome complement that have a limited geographic distribution. These are related to, and probably ancestral to, a more recent and widespread species with a greater number of chromosomes. One patroendemic of the lily family is *Calochortus umbellatus* (2n =20); its probable descendant is *C. uniflorus* (2n = 20, 40) (Stebbins and Major 1965).

In contrast, apoendemics are defined as geographically-limited species with a chromosome complement greater than normal. Such a species either appears together with or adjacent to a more widely distributed species bearing fewer sets of chromosomes than the species from which it is likely descended. Lily apoendemic pairs include *Allium cratericola* (2n = 28) and *A. obtusum* (2n = 14), and *Calochortus vestae* (2n = 28) and *C. luteus* (2n = 14).

Many rare species in California and elsewhere are restricted to specific soil types, and as such, are considered "edaphic endemics."

In California, an often toxic soil generally called "serpentinite" is characterized by an imbalance of several essential nutrients and an oft-times lethal availability of toxic metals, such as chromium and nickel. California's "serpentine" plants are well known worldwide, and many of these are rare. Familiar rare lily examples include a variety of onions and mariposa lilies, including *Allium sanbornii, A. jepsonii,* and *Calochortus obispoensis.*

In summary, there are many reasons why lilies species are rare in California, and likely as many ideas about why any single lily species might be rare. Only infrequently does a single "cause" by itself truly explain why a species is rare. And although some taxa are rare because of one particular aspect of their biology, such as poor seed dispersal, and still others may be rare because they are old and "on their way out," it is premature to generalize about why all plant species are rare. It is important, therefore, to understand the biology of a rare species, to know its evolutionary history, and to understand current threats to its habitat. Only with such knowledge can rare lilies in California have much better chances for long-term survival.

P R O T E C T I O N   O F   R A R E   P L A N T S   I N   C A L I F O R N I A

Rare plants in California can usually be afforded at least two forms of legal protection. At the highest jurisdictional level is federal protection as an "endangered" or "threatened" species as designated under the Endangered Species of Act (ESA) of 1973, as amended. The U.S. Fish and Wildlife Service (USFWS) is given regulatory authority to designate endangered and threatened species that need protection from extinction under the auspices of the federal government. Section 3 of the Endangered Species Act defines endangered as any species, including subspecies "in danger of extinction throughout all or a signficant portion of its range." A threatened species is defined as a species "likely to become an endangered species within the foreseeable future throughout all or a significant portion of its range." Therefore, to be "federally listed" as endangered or threatened indicates that the species has undergone a public review process typically initiated by the U.S. Fish and Wildlife Service Office of

Endangered Species to receive protection under the U.S. Endangered Species Act. No lilies in California are currently listed as endangered or threatened under the ESA.

The second level of legal protection is provided by state laws. The legal framework for rare, threatened, and endangered plants in California includes the California Environmental Quality Act of 1970 (CEQA), Native Plant Protection Act of 1977 (NPPA), California Endangered Species Act of 1984 (CESA), and the Natural Communities Conservation Planning Act of 1991 (NCCPA). Most relevant is the CESA, a legislative extension of the NPPA which, when enacted, greatly enhanced the state's legal protection for vascular plants. Specifically, CESA designated "endangered" and "threatened" categories, and added the category "rare." A plant is considered endangered by the state of California if "its prospects of survival and reproduction are in immediate jeopardy from one or more causes." Rare lilies given the state's endangered designation include four species of *Brodiaea* (*B. coronaria* ssp. *rosea*, *B. filifolia*, *B. insignis*, and *B. pallida*); one fritillary (*F. roderickii*); two *Lilium* species (*L. occidentale* and *L. pitkinense*), and the Dehesa nolina.

CESA defines a threatened native plant as one that "although not presently threatened with extinction, is likely to become an endangered species in the foreseeable future in the absence of the special protection and management efforts." Munz's onion and the Tiburon mariposa lily are the only California state-listed threatened lilies today. A rare plant as defined by CESA is one that "although not presently threatened with extinction, it is in such small numbers throughout its range that it may become endangered if its present environment worsens." The five rare lilies listed under CESA as rare include the Yosemite onion (*Allium yosemitense*), dwarf goldenstar, Dunn's mariposa (*Calochortus dunnii*), Siskiyou mariposa lily (*Calochortus persistens*), and the Camatta Canyon amole (*Chlorogalum purpureum* var. *reductum*).

An additional level of protection given to rare plants in California is that provided by the California Native Plant Society (CNPS). The CNPS is an extraordinarily influential organization of lay and professional botanists united by their interest in California plants and dedicated to the protection of the California flora. This group has published a listing—*Inventory of Rare and Endangered Vascular Plants in California*—now in its fifth edition (Skinner and Pavlik 1994), that serves as a compendium of California's rare, threatened, and endangered plants, as well as those that may soon be listed by the state or federal government. The current *Inventory* maintains four lists. List 1A includes all species that are presumed extinct in California. The Single-flowered mariposa Lily (*Calochortus monanthus*) is such a species. List 1B, as represented by the majority of our rare lilies, includes rare or endangered taxa in California and elsewhere. Taxa that are designated rare or endangered in California, but are more common elsewhere are found on the CNPS's List 2. Rare lilies found on List 2 include Shaw's agave (*Agave shawii*), the Great Basin onion (*Allium atrorubens* var. *atrorubens*), and small-flowered androstephium (*Androstephium breviflorum*), as well as a few others. Although no rare lilies in California are found on List 3, this list includes plants about which we need more information to assess their degree of endangerment. Finally, List 4 includes those plants with a limited distribution, but are not sufficiently restricted to warrant official listing. A significant number of rare Californian lilies are on this final list, including Utah agave (*Agave utahensis*), Mt. Pinos onion (*Allium howellii* var. *clokey*), Catalina mariposa lily (*Calochortus catalinae*), lemon-colored fawn lily (*Erythronium citrinum* var. *citrinum*), and Trinity Mountains triteleia (*Triteleia crocea* var. *modesta*), as well as several others.

It should be recognized that unique populations (e.g., morphologically, genetically, or physiologically distinct populations often found at the periphery of a species' range) may represent new, undescribed taxa that are not protected by federal or state laws. In short, unless a population has formally been recognized as a taxon by the botanical community, various levels of government jurisdiction do not afford legal protection. Populations in which unique events (e.g., chromosomal mutations) are evident should be watched closely by those interested in conservation, precisely because it is within these populations that new forms typically are generated. If California is to remain notable for its diverse and rapidly evolving flora, then we must work toward the preservation of not just "listed" taxa, but toward the preservation of unique populations so that our flora can continue to evolve in spite of of rapid human population expansion within our borders.

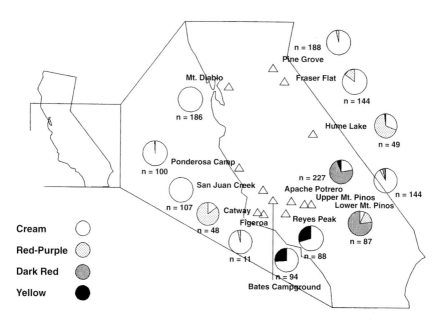

Figure 3.1. Proportion of color morphs in each population of Calochortus venustus *studied (n = sample size). Modified and reprinted with permission from R. Zebell.*

Chapter 3

PATTERNS OF LILY EVOLUTION AND ECOLOGY IN CALIFORNIA

Important research on certain of the more showy lilies in California has documented paradigmatic patterns of vascular plant evolution and pollination ecology. In this regard, lilies have proven to be ideal organisms with which to test theories about chromosomal evolution (Ness, Soltis, and Soltis 1990), selection pressures and the evolution of new breeding systems and floral syndromes (Skinner 1988), population dynamics (Fiedler 1987, Fredricks 1992, Knapp 1996), and the evolutionary and taxonomic limits of morphologically complex taxa (Zebell 1993). Brief discussion of two such examples follows. Each independently illustrates some element of the evolutionary patterns and trends that are found in the California Liliaceae; together, and more importantly, they emphasize the importance of evolutionary and ecological research in the management and conservation of rare lily taxa.

PATTERNS OF FLORAL EVOLUTION

CALOCHORTUS

Background. The genus *Calochortus* is distinguished from other Liliaceae by its short (or absent) style, sepaloid outer perianth whorl, septicidal capsules, embryology (i.e., polygonum-type embryo sac formation), and a chromosome number that is never n = 12. Twelve is the base number for other members of the family tribe, *Tulipae*, to which *Calochortus* historically has been assigned. *Calochortus* has also been considered a monotypic family, the Calochortaceae, by many botanists. Suggestions regarding its sister group (i.e., closest botanical relative) include tulips (*Tulipa*), fetid adder's tongue (*Scoliopus*), fawn lilies (*Erythronium*), *Lloydia*, and toad lilies (*Tricyrtis*). It is evident, therefore, that the evolutionary relationships of *Calochortus* are problematic!

As delimited by the most recent monograph (Ownbey 1940), *Calochortus* is divided into three taxonomic sections. Ownbey's work is significant in that it was the first complete treatise to clearly distinguish and articulate three suites of characteristics within this rather large lily genus. While the monograph is now out of date and incomplete, largely because many new taxa have been described since 1940 and some do not readily fit into Ownbey's taxonomy, the monograph remains the logical starting place for anyone interested in the genus.

As described in the monograph, Section *Calochortus* comprises the globe lilies, fairy lanterns, pussy ears, and various other members which are distinguished primarily by bulb coat and fruit characteristics. This section is restricted largely to California, with its center of diversity on the Klamath Plateau. Many rare species are found within section *Calochortus*, particularly endemics in northern California and rare serpentine species of southern Oregon.

Section *Mariposa* includes all true "mariposa lilies," and clearly represents a natural group. The center of diversity for the mariposa lilies is considered to be the Transverse Ranges, an area of striking geologic complexity. Members are distinguished by their three-angled fruits and membranaceous bulb coat. Over forty years ago it was suggested by the California botanist, Robert F. Hoover, that the mariposa lilies be given generic status, a suggestion based on leaf shape and persistence, stigma position, seed coat, and chromosome number. Current nomenclature does not follow this proposition, however. Several species of mariposa lilies are widespread (e.g., *Calochortus venustus*, *C. luteus*, *C. superbus*), and several are now increasingly restricted geographically, despite a formerly widespread distribution (e.g., *Calochortus catalinae*).

Section *Cyclobothra* is represented by only a few members in California, as its main distribution is along the Sierra Madre Mountains of Mexico. Taxa in this section bear three-angled fruits and a reticulate bulb coat. A significant number of California's *Cyclobothra* are rare. For example, *Calochortus obispoensis* is restricted to less than ten localized populations in the Santa Lucia Mountains along the central coast of California.

Floral Variation and Taxonomic Limits in *Calochortus venustus* (Zebell 1993). *Calochortus venustus*, the Venus mariposa lily, is one of the most widespread and lovely of all the mariposa lilies. It is a member of section *Mariposa*, subsection *Venusti*, which is distinguished by the presence of a membranaceous bulb coat, three-angled fruit, obscurely monochasial subumbellate inflorescences, anthers lacking sagittate bases, and nectaries (glands) that lack membranes and that are neither depressed nor oblong, but are covered by short, moderately thick hairs. Other species in the *Venusti* complex include *C. argillosus*, *C. catalinae*, *C. dunnii*, *C. flexuosus*, *C. leichtlinii*, *C. luteus*, *C. simulans*, *C. splendens*, *C. superbus*, and *C. vestae*.

The Venus mariposa lily is highly variable in flower color throughout its relatively broad geographic range. Flowers range from a creamy white, yellow, pink, purple, and orange, to dark red. In addition, each flower may bear one or two spots, or be striated, mottled, solidly colored, or swirled. In the past, many of these color forms were given infraspecific status (e.g., *C. venustus* var. *purpurescens*, *C. venustus* var. *sanguineus*, etc.). However, until the work of Zebell (1993), no research was initiated to clarify this bewildering array of floral patterns. Observational records (Purdy 1901) suggested that flowers in the Coast Ranges always bore two spots, and that Coast Range petals of the Venus mariposa lily were wider than they were long. In addition, flowers from Sierra Nevada populations of *Calochortus venustus* were presumed to be missing the distal spot, colors were presumed richer than those found in Coast Range flowers, and petals were relatively longer than they were wide.

Zebell (1993) systematically examined the variability of color morphs, spot patterns, and petal shape throughout the range of *Calochortus venustus* (and two other closely related mariposa lilies) to assess whether any of the color morphs were sufficiently distinct to warrant taxonomic recognition. He collected 1570 flowers from thirteen locations throughout the lily's geographic range, and assessed flower spotting patterns and flower color with the use of a standardized color chart. Zebell documented four consistent and widespread color morphs. "Creamy white" is most frequent (72%) flower color of the Venus mariposa lily, followed distantly by "dark red" (15%), "red-purple" (8%), and "yellow" (4%) (Figure 3.1). Several other flower colors are found in this species, such as "orange-yellow" or intermediates of cream and red-purple, but these were determined not sufficiently unique to warrant distinction.

Interestingly, the distribution of flower colors is not equal—that is to say, not all flower color forms can be found in each population. All populations have at least one cream flower, but only six of the thirteen populations studied had a red-purple flower, five had at least one yellow flower, and only three populations had a dark red flower (Figure 3.1). Thus, while dark red is proportionately the second most common flower color produced throughout the range of populations of *C. venustus*, this flower color is found in only three different populations out of all those studied.

Petal spot patterns were equally interesting. All but two of the thirteen population's had flowers bearing spots. The unusual "spotless" populations are found in the Transverse Ranges where floral variation in the Venus mariposa lily is particularly complex, and where the populations support a higher proportion of dark red flowers in which the spotting is not evident. Of the spotted populations, over 75% of the populations consist of two-spotted flowers (Figure 3.2). While Purdy's (1901) observations were not borne out, a slight trend does exist in the Sierra Nevada. Populations in the north have proportionately more individuals with one spot, and those in the south support proportionally more individuals with two spots.

The research of Zebell (1993) also addressed the question of variable petal and gland shapes. To document this pattern of flower variation, Zebell analyzed the petal and gland shape using a computer-assisted image capturing system. Specifically, a mounted video camera captured petal images from a light table, shunting the image as a video signal to a TV monitor which displayed the image. The video image was then converted into digital information and stored on a computer.

Thirteen petal and gland distance variables were measured to assess size and shape variation. Sixty-two flower samples were collected from twenty-five locations, and each petal flower was digitized to capture petal and gland contours. Results from this portion of the

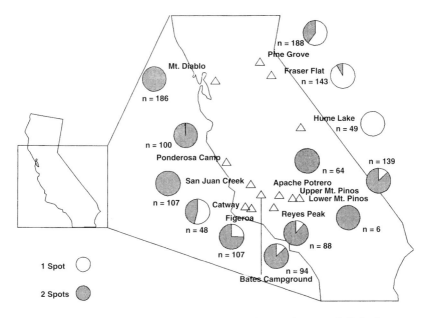

Figure 3.2. Proportion of petal spots in each population of Calochortus venustus *studied (n = sample size). Modified and reprinted with permission from R. Zebell.*

study were striking. All of the populations exhibit great morphological variability in both petal and gland shape (Figure 3.3). In virtually every instance, petals from a single population range from being strongly "clawed" and wider than long, to being distinctly wedge-shaped with a truncated, flat, distal petal margin, to being nearly elliptic with a gradually rounded distal margin. Gland shapes vary from being round, to elongate and rectangular, to square, to crescent-shaped, to "mustached," to an inverted V, or to M-shaped.

Petal and gland shape data of *C. venustus* were then subjected to a multivariate statistical analysis, along with data obtained for two additional and closely related rare species, *C. argillosus* and *C. simulans*. Results from this portion of Zebell's work documented distinct species boundaries for the three taxa, suggesting that despite many superficial similarities and great within-species and within-population variation, the three mariposa lilies are sufficiently different from each other to warrant distinct specific status.

To summarize this impressive work, color forms and spot patterns of the Venus mariposa lily were not found by Zebell (1993) to be either ecologically or geographically separable throughout the species' range. Petal and gland shapes also exhibited great within-population variation, but overall, the Venus mariposa lily is a distinct and distinctive taxon within the genus. Such extreme variation below the level of species is exceptional, even unparalleled in this large western lily genus, but no clear patterns nor trends are consistent enough to warrant infraspecific recognition.

The *Calochortus venustus* study raises important issues that are not easily addressed in conservation biology. The great floral variation shown by the Venus mariposa lily is a clear example of the tremendous diversity that often exists within wide-ranging plant species, in California and elsewhere. Populations not only hold a wide range of different floral morphs, but each population is a bit different from the next. However, current state and federal endangered species statutes do not clearly protect unusual plant populations, particularly for wide ranging species. Thus it is incumbent upon all botanists and interested laypersons to be cognizant of the great diversity that exists in our many of our common lilies. If we as conservationists can clearly document and articulate the uniqueness of these lily taxa, as Zebell (1993) has so elegantly done, we can more effectively accomplish the protection of these unique lilies.

P A T T E R N S   O F   P O L L I N A T I O N   E C O L O G Y

L I L I U M

Background. *Lilium* consists of approximately one hundred species distributed circumboreally. Approximately twenty-one species of *Lilium* are found in the western United States, and of these, eight occur west of the Rocky Mountains. Skinner (1988) suggests that there are a total of seventeen taxa (species and their infraspecific entities) in this region, while other authors posit a more liberal accounting of taxa (e.g., Ballantyne 1978) for Pacific coast *Lilium*.

The genus has a long history of taxonomic classification. Early efforts relied primarily on the variation in floral form (Skinner 1988), and thus four subgenera have long been recognized. Subgenus *Eulirion* holds the species with funnel-shaped flowers, while *Archelirion* is a subgenus that was erected for the lilies with more or less horizontal flowers and broad, bell-shaped perianths. The remaining two sub-genera are *Isolirion*, established for the erect lilies that bear clawed perianth segments, and subgenus *Martagon*, perhaps the most famil-iar lilies with pendent flowers, strongly recurved perianth segments, and divergent stamens. These latter lilies are often known as "turk's caps."

Floral Variation and Pollination Ecology in *Lilium* (Skin-ner 1988). *Lilium* is an unmistakably distinctive genus of perennial herbs, remarkably diverse in its floral patterns, particularly the myriad permutations of floral form, shape, and color. The resulting variety of *Lilium* flowers has led to a great richness of pollination syndromes and animal pollinators. In an extraordinary doctoral dissertation, Dr. Mark Skinner (1988) described the floral features of thirteen species of *Lilium* found in the western United States, and demonstrated how those floral features govern patterns of lily pollination. Skinner fo-cused on five aspects of floral variation within the western North American representatives of the genus: (a) description of the broad

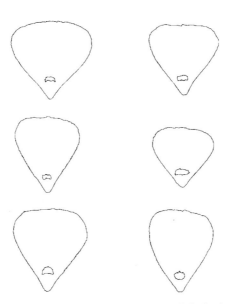

Figure 3.3. Selected petal and gland contours of Calochortus venustus *collected from Pine Grove, Amador County. Reprinted with permission from R. Zebell.*

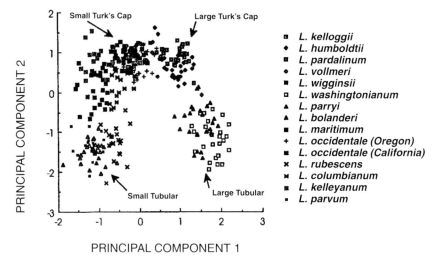

Figure 3.4. Scores on the first two principal components for 326 Lilium *flowers delimiting four morphologies of Western lilies. Principal Component 1 (PC1) summarizes flower size variables and Principal Component 2 (PC2) summarizes one set of flower shape variables. Modified and reprinted with permission from M. Skinner.*

variation in *Lilium* floral morphology using multivariate statistics; (b) *Lilium* floral biology as it relates to breeding systems; (c) patterns of nectar secretion and its regulating factors; (d) comparative *Lilium* pollination ecology; and (d) a phylogenetic systematic analysis of floral evolution in North American *Lilium* taxa.

In the first volume of Skinner's work, statistical analyses on a set of morphological variables were performed on 330 individuals from fifteen taxa. In contrast to the computerized image-capturing devise employed by Zebell, Skinner recorded all morphological measures on live plants in the field, using either a hand-held ruler or dial calipers where appropriate. Results from this portion of Skinner's research revealed four flower morphologies: large and small "turk's-cap," and large and small tubular (Figure 3.4). *Lilium parryi* and *L. washingtonianum* represent the only true lilies classified as "large-tubular," while *L. bolanderi, L. maritimum, L. parvum,* and *L. rubescens* represent the "small-tubular" floral morphs. The majority of the western species of *Lilium* therefore are considered "turk's-caps": *L. humboldtii* and *L. pardalinum* are large and *L. columbianum, L. kelloggii,*

L. kelleyanum, *L. occidentale* (Oregon and California populations), *L. vollmeri*, and *L. wigginsii* are small.

A particularly insightful chapter of Skinner (1988) addresses the pollination ecology of western *Lilium* taxa. Skinner suggests that a "pollination syndrome mythology" (Skinner 1988, p. 215) has evolved in floral biology circles, whereby few if any systematic analyses have tested whether or not certain floral characteristics, such as flower color, nectar constituency, time of flower opening, etc., are truly involved in effecting pollination. Skinner exhaustively analyzed the distribution of floral features presumably important in the attraction of animal pollinators to western true lilies, and compared these floral features against his (and others') observed patterns of pollination.

Somewhat surprisingly, pollination patterns are not completely dictated by floral morphology, as might be expected from theory alone. Timing and amount of nectar secretion determines to some extent patterns of animal visition. Lily morphology does, however, determine the broader syndrome of pollination. Large-tubular *Lilium* species are pollinated by hawkmoths (Sphingidae [*Hyles*, *Sphinx*]); small tubular species are pollinated by either hummingbirds (Anna, Black-chinned, Calliope, Rufus, and Allen) and/or bees, including bumblebees (*Bombus* spp.); and both large and small turk's-cap lilies are pollinated primarily by a diverse mix of large butterflies, primarily the swallowtails (Papilionidae [*Papilio*, *Speyeria*, *Parnassius*]) and Nymphalidae (*Danaus*). Turk's cap lilies are pollinated by hummingbirds as well, but to a much less extent.

Skinner determined that interspecific patterns of floral orientation (i.e., variation of flower angle) are best interpreted as adaptations that have evolved to increase the foraging efficiency of the major pollinators, as well as to increase the deposition of *Lilium* pollen on those pollinators. Specifically, evolutionarily more recent pollination syndromes (e.g., horizontal, small-tubular flowers) suggest a progression from an ancestral pendulent orientation toward a horizontal one, depending upon the flower's reliance on hovering pollinators. Hummingbirds, for example, likely prefer horizontally-oriented lilies; moth-pollinated flowers are also more or less horizontal, which is a feature related to the preferred foraging orientation of sphingid moths.

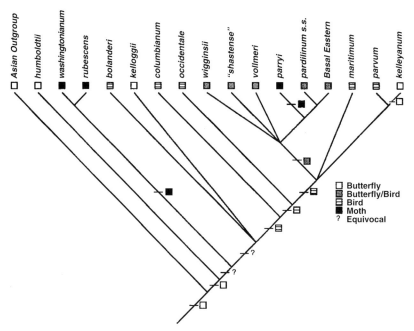

Figure 3.5. Phylogenetic hypothesis of the evolution of pollination syndromes in the Lilium *species of California. Data analysis involved twenty morphometric variables sampled from 330 individuals of fifteen taxa. Modified and reprinted with permission from M. Skinner.*

Small, tubular flowers of the "small-tubular" *Lilium* morph are most effectively pollinated when the floral tube length is approximately equal to the combined bill and tongue length of the hummingbird, but this is not true for the "turk's-cap" *Lilium* morphs. These taxa bear more pendulent flowers efficient at depositing pollen on butterfly visitors. Turk's-cap flowers only partially exclude hummingbirds and as a consequence of a poor fit, are inefficient at depositing pollen on hummingbirds. Skinner (1988, p. 314) warily suggests that a "unilateral floral evolution has clearly occurred in several western lilies to match nectar tubes to swallowtail tongues. . . ."

The concluding section of Skinner (1988) presents a series of phylogenetic hypotheses concerning the evolution of floral features and the pollination syndromes for western *Lilium* species. Using a cladistic (phylogenetic) analysis that included twenty-two morphological and cytological characters, Skinner's work (1988) suggests that the two large tubular lily species evolved independently from the turk's-cap lineage, as did the small tubular lilies. The analyses also revealed strong parallelism (i.e., independent evolution) in the evolution of flower morphology, orientation, color, scent, and the timing, amount, and location of nectar secretion. One of the more intriguing but elusive results of the cladistic analyses is the possibility that North America turk's-cap *Lilium* species have evolved from the turk's-cap ancestors that were pollinated not by butterflies, but by hummingbirds (Figure 3.5). Such taxa include *L. kelleyanum* and the *L. pardalinum* complex, excluding *L. parryi*.

Skinner (1988:iv) concluded:

> *During shifts in pollination mode, the fine tuning of flower color lags behind initial evolutionary modification of reward structure [nectar] but, as with flower morphology, eventually evolves to complement the sensory and behavioral characteristics of major pollinators. In western lilies, floral morphology evolves to maximize pollen deposition by the flower visitors that pollinate most effectively.*

The studies of Zebell, Skinner, and other lily researchers demonstrate the importance of lilies in understanding broader patterns of floral variation. Such patterns can elucidate evolutionary trends in the more conspicuous and lovely members of the western North American flora, i.e., the Liliaceae. Further work can only lead to a more thorough understanding of this distinctive family of monocots in California as well as worldwide. With this knowledge, the scientific, horticultural, and cultural significance of the lily family will not go unappreciated nor unprotected.

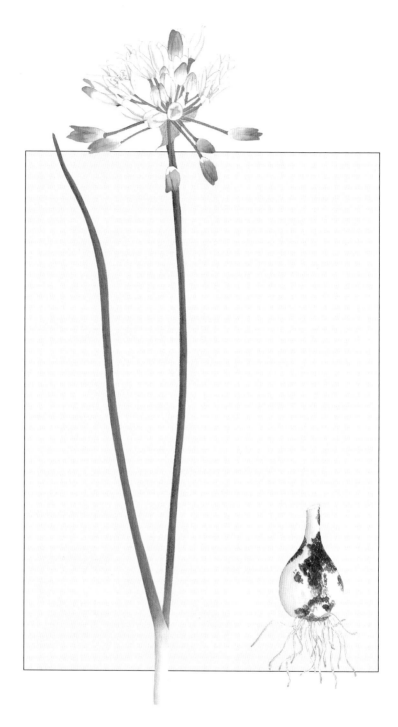

Allium fimbriatum

VAR. *munzii*

PLATE 1

Chapter 4
PLATE TEXT

Allium munzii

ALLIUM MUNZII (TRAUB) D. McNEAL
(MUNZ'S ONION)

Munz's onion belongs to an alliance of species related to *Allium sanbornii*, one of nine North American alliances in the genus *Allium*. Species in the *Allium sanbornii* alliance are distinguished by a single leaf per bulb and two prominent, flattened structures near the summit of each ovary lobe that form a six-parted ovarian crest. Recent taxonomic work has elevated six varieties of *Allium fimbriatum*, of which *A. munzii* was one, to specific status in an attempt to clarify the extremely confusing taxonomic relationships among the *Allium fimbriatum* taxa.

Munz's onion is known from fewer than ten populations, being restricted to grassy openings in the coastal sage scrub of Riverside County. *Allium munzii* is threatened by the rapid urbanization of Southern California as well as by mining, agriculture, and the invasion of non-native plant species. It is listed as a federally-proposed endangered species, a state-listed threatened species, and is on list 1B of the California Native Plant Society's *Inventory of Rare and Endangered Plants Inventory* (Skinner and Pavlik 1994). Populations of Munz's onion on the Cleveland National Forest also are afforded additional protection, as it is listed as a U.S. Forest Service "sensitive species."

Allium sanbornii

A L L I U M   S A N B O R N I I   A L P H .   W O O D   V A R .   S A N B O R N I I

(S A N B O R N ' S   O N I O N)

Sanborn's onion is one of two varieties of *Allium sanbornii*, both of which are uncommon in California. The two taxa are found in the foothills of the Sierra Nevada from Butte County southward to Mariposa County, and at various locations in Tehama County extending northward to Oregon. The two infraspecific taxa are distinguished primarily by their stigma shape, anther color, and flowering times.

Other species in the *"Allium sanbornii* complex" include two additional rare onions, Jepson's onion *(Allium jepsonii)* and Rawhide Hill onion *(Allium tuolumnense)*. Recently, the taxonomy and evolutionary history of this difficult group has been clarified, although it is a complex taxonomic group that historically has been much misunderstood by botanists.

Sanborn's onion can be found in scattered, generally small populations on serpentinite outcrops in the Sierra Nevada foothills at the northern extent of the Sacramento Valley, from Shasta County to Calaveras County. *Allium sanbornii* var. *sanbornii* also has been collected from a single population in southern Oregon. Sanborn's onion is afforded no federal or state protection, but can be found on the California Native Plant Society's *Inventory* List 4.

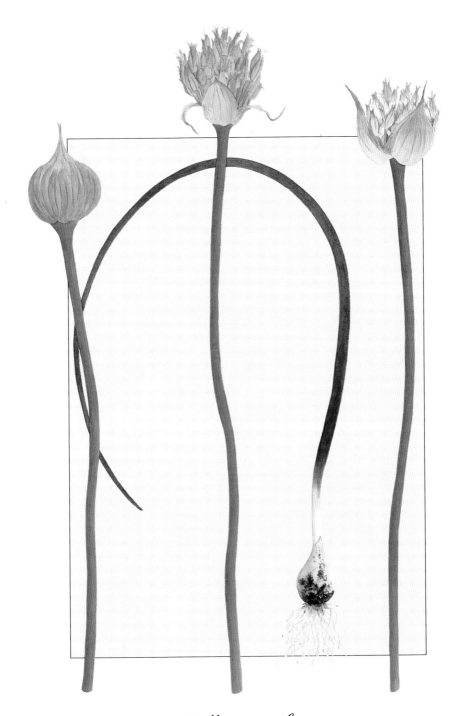

Allium sanbornii

VAR. *sanbornii*

PLATE 3

Allium shevockii

ALLIUM SHEVOCKII D. MCNEAL

SPANISH NEEDLE ONION

Spanish Needle onion is a rare species only recently discovered. It is considered closely related to Sanborn's onion. *Allium shevockii* consists of only two known populations, both restricted to Spanish Needle Peak, a mountaintop in the remote regions of northeastern Kern County. The unusual habitat of this rare onion consists of soil pockets within metamorphic outcrops and steep talus slopes between 2000 and 2500 meters. *Allium shevockii* bulbs occur primarily along the margins of these rock outcrops where the slope is relatively more stable. Although it has showy crimson flowers, it appears to reproduce only rarely by seed. *Allium shevockii* is named after Mr. James Shevock, regional botanist for the U.S. Forest Service, Region V, and an expert on the flora of the Sierra Nevada. It can be found on the California Native Plant Society's *Inventory* List 1B.

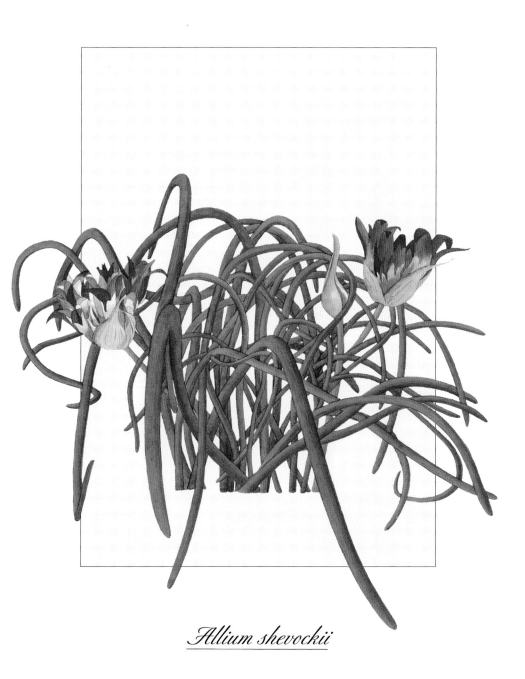

Allium shevockii

Allium yosemitense

A L L I U M   Y O S E M I T E N S E   E A S T W O O D

(Y O S E M I T E   O N I O N)

Yosemite onion is restricted to the central Sierra Nevada at elevations ranging from 800 to 2200 meters. As a rare species, it is geographically restricted and known from fewer than twenty populations, most of which are inaccessible. As a result, botanists know very little about the Yosemite onion, although it can be found in cultivation, primarily in California's public botanical gardens. Despite the paucity of information about this *Allium* species, *Allium yosemitense* is a state-listed rare species and can be found on the California Native Plant Society's *Inventory* List 1B.

Allium yosemitense

PLATE 5

Bloomeria humilis

BLOOMERIA HUMILIS HOOVER

(DWARF GOLDENSTAR)

Bloomeria is a genus named after H.G. Bloomer, an early San Francisco botanist and former curator of botany at the California Academy of Sciences. The genus consists of only two species, *B. crocea*, the common goldenstar, and *B. humilis*, the dwarf goldenstar. Both species range from central and southern California into northern Baja California, Mexico. *Bloomeria* looks superficially much like *Allium* and *Muilla*, but unlike either genus, each anther filament bears a cuplike appendage at its base.

Dwarf goldenstar is a rare lily known only from two populations in the Arroyo de la Cruz region of San Luis Obispo County. It prefers open grasslands and chaparral edges within this region. Some botanists believed, however, that the range of this rare lily may extend into southern Monterey County when further field surveys are made. *Bloomeria humilis* is a state-listed rare species and a California Native Plant Society *Inventory* List 1B species. It was recently reclassified by the U.S. Fish and Wildlife Service and is no longer a federal candidate rare species.

Bloomeria humilis

PLATE 6

Brodiaea coronaria

BRODIAEA CORONARIA
(SALISBURY) ENGLER
SSP. *ROSEA* (E. GREENE) T. NIEHAUS

(INDIAN VALLEY BRODIAEA)

Indian Valley brodiaea differs from its sister subspecies, *Brodiaea coronaria* ssp. *coronaria,* in that its slightly smaller flowers are rose to light pink in color, the tips of the pollen chambers are rounded (not hooked), the staminodia are often pink, and the corm coat is rather thin and fibrous. *Brodiaea coronaria* ssp. *rosea* is a member of section *Coronariae* as its name suggests. This rare lily is restricted to serpentinite grasslands in Tehama, Lake, and Glenn Counties of the North Coast Range. Like many species of *Brodiaea,* the Indian Valley brodiaea is easy to grow and presently is in cultivation. *Brodiaea coronoria* ssp. *rosea* is listed as endangered by the state of California and is found on the California Native Plant Society's *Inventory* List 1B.

Brodiaea coronaria

SSP. *rosea*

Brodiaea insignis

B R O D I A E A   I N S I G N I S   (J E P S O N)
T .   N I E H A U S

(K A W E A H   B R O D I A E A)

The Kaweah brodiaea is known from approximately twenty populations in the watersheds of the Tule and Kaweah Rivers. This species is a member of section *Stellares* and is distinguished by its rose to pink-purple perianth and by staminodia that are held close to the functional stamens. Although this rare lily is not often encountered in the wild, it can be found in cultivation. Like the Indian Valley brodiaea, *Brodiaea insignis* is listed as endangered by the state of California and is found on List 1B of the CNPS *Inventory*. Currently the species is threatened by residential development, road maintenance, grazing by domestic livestock, and the invasion of non-native species.

Brodiaea insignis

Calochortus albus

C A L O C H O R T U S   A L B U S   B E N T H A M
V A R .   R U B E L L U S   E .   G R E E N E

(R O S Y   F A I R Y   L A N T E R N)

The rosy fairy lantern is not currently recognized by the botanical community as a distinct variety of the widely distributed White fairy lantern, largely because intermediate color forms exist sporadically thoughout the central California coast. However, further taxonomic work is needed to determine the validity of its infraspecific status. Fairy lanterns belong to section *Calochortus*, one of three sections in this genus of approximately seventy taxa.

The deep pink flowers of the rosy fairy lantern as depicted in Plate 8 can be found only in a few isolated populations in southern Monterey County and northern San Luis Obispo County. Superficially *C. albus* var. *rubellus* resembles the common species *Calochortus amoenus*, but this latter species is restricted to the foothills of the southern Sierra Nevada, and therefore does not occur in the Coast Ranges. In addition, gland position and petal color differ considerably between the two. Because *Calochortus albus* var. *rubellus* is not currently accepted as a distinct taxonomic entity, the rosy-flowered populations of *Calochortus albus* do not have any legally protected status.

Calochortus albus
VAR. *rubellus*

Calochortus argillosus

C A L O C H O R T U S   A R G I L L O S U S   (H O O V E R)
R .   Z E B E L L   &   P .   F I E D L E R

(C L A Y   M A R I P O S A   L I L Y)

The lay mariposa lily was originally described as *Mariposa argillosa* in 1944 by the California botanist, Dr. Robert F. Hover, when he attempted to segregate the new genus *Mariposa* from the genus *Calochortus*. Although not recognized currently by researchers of this group, the mariposa lilies are distinctively different from the other species of *Calochortus*, and are placed in their own section, *Mariposa*.

Hoover considered *Calochortus argillosus* distinct from the Venus mariposa lily (*Calochortus venustus*) primarily because of the clay mariposa's more strongly bulbiferous habit, a transversely-elongated nectary, and the distinctly stout capsule. Unless one is familiar with the variability of the forms and colors of *C. venustus*, however, the two species are easily confused. Recently, *Calochortus* researchers clarified the name for *Calochortus argillosus* and have stressed its rare and localized status. Because of this recent valid publication, legally protected status is now being considered.

Calochortus argillosus has two distinct groups—a coastal form in central San Luis Obispo County and an interior form in the Santa Clara Valley and southward. These two groups are distinguished largely by floral morphology and color pattern differences. The coastal form as depicted in Plate 9 is largely invariable with regard to its color patterning. The interior form, however, is remarkably variable in both color pattern, and in petal and gland shape. Further field research will clarify this beautiful but confusing mariposa lily.

Calochortus argillosus

Calochortus clavatus

CALOCHORTUS CLAVATUS S. WATSON
SSP. CLAVATUS

(CLUB-HAIRED MARIPOSA LILY)

The club-haired mariposa lily exhibits a wide range in vegetative morphology and in floral coloration and patterning throughout its geographic distribtution. Major variants are given taxonomic recognition, and virtually all rare forms are restricted to specific geographic settings in the state. *Calochortus clavatus* ssp. *clavatus*, for example, grows largely in heavy clay soils, often serpeninite-derived, and mostly in the Santa Lucia Mountains of the Central Coast Range and in the Sierra Nevada foothills of El Dorado County. It is considered to be the stoutest-stemmed, tallest, and largest-flowered of all species of *Calochortus*. In addition, the stem is characteristically zig-zag in appearance. Its specific epithet, *clavatus*, refers to the club-shaped hairs surrounding the nectary. Formerly more widespread than evidenced by its current distribution, *C. clavatus* ssp. *clavatus* is threatened by habitat loss, agricultural conversion, and urban expansion. It is placed in the California Native Plant Society's *Inventory* List 4.

Calochortus clavatus

SSP. *clavatus*

PLATE 11

Calochortus clavatus

CALOCHORTUS CLAVATUS S. WATSON
SSP. RECURVIFOLIUS (HOOVER) MUNZ
(ARROYO DE LA CRUZ MARIPOSA LILY)

The Arroyo de la Cruz mariposa lily is known from fewer than ten locations in the Arroyo de la Cruz region of San Luis Obispo County. This variety of *C. clavatus* is a distinctive mariposa lily in that its leaves strongly recurve upon the plant, giving each individual an unusual curly appearance. Virtually nothing is known about *C. clavatus* ssp. *recurvifolius*, although it is a California Native Plant Society *Inventory* List 1B species.

Calochortus clavatus

SSP. *recurvifolius*

PLATE 12

Calochortus obispoensis

CALOCHORTUS OBISPOENSIS LEMMON

(SAN LUIS MARIPOSA LILY)

Calochortus obispoensis is one of the most distinctive of all mariposa lilies. Its flowers are greatly reduced in size and profusely bearded with yellow and dark-red hairs. The San Luis mariposa lily belongs to section *Cyclobothra* and therefore is more closely allied to its southern California and Mexican relatives (e.g., *C. weedii*) than other *Calochortus* species found throughout the central coast of California. The San Luis mariposa lily is restricted to serpentinite coastal bluffs and hillsides of the San Lucia Moutains in San Luis Obispo County.

Calochortus obispoensis is a geographically-restricted endemic, currently threatened by grazing, road construction, and recreational activities. Recent research on the population biology of this rare lily suggests that several populations may be in decline. Despite this research and the serious threats to its habitat, the San Luis mariposa lily is considered too common for formal protection by state and federal governments, but it is on List 1B of the California Native Plant Society's *Inventory of Rare and Endangered Plants of California* (Skinner and Pavlik 1994).

Calochortus obispoensis

Calochortus persistens

C A L O C H O R T U S   P E R S I S T E N S   F .   O W N B E Y

(S I S K I Y O U   M A R I P O S A   L I L Y)

The Siskiyou mariposa lily belongs to section *Calochortus* and is distinguished by its persistent perianth, as the specific epithet suggests. It is an odd member of its subsection (*Nitidi*), as the capsule is pendant, not erect, as in the other members of this taxonomic group. Like many other species of *Calochortus*, this species is very localized in distribution. The Siskiyou mariposa lily is found in small populations within the Siskiyou Mountains near Yreka, California.

Calochortus persistens currently is threatened by various forms of habitat disturbance and by the invasion of non-native species. It is, however, found on the Klamath National Forest, and therefore is a listed "sensitive species" by the U.S. Forest Service. The Siskiyou mariposa lily also is listed as a California rare species and is on List 1B of the California Native Plant Society's *Inventory*.

Calochortus persistens

PLATE 14

Calochortus pulchellus

The Mt. Diablo fairy lantern is a member of section *Calochortus*, and with its closely related sister species, *C. albus*, *C. amoenus*, *C. amabilis*, and *C. raichei*, form the natural species complex, subsection *Pulchelli*. All are characterized in part by nodding flowers and fruit. Three taxa, *C. pulchellus*, *C. amabilis*, and *C. raichei*, are yellow-flowered species of taxonomically distinctive, but slightly varying color hues. *Calchortus albus* is typically white, with pink-flowered forms occasionally found (see Plate 1). *Calochortus amoenus* is a lovely rosy pink and is geographically distant from the all other members of subsection *Pulchelli* except *C. albus*.

As its common name suggests, the Mt. Diablo fairy lantern is endemic to Mt. Diablo, a geological landmark at the terminus of the Diablo Range in Contra Costa County. *Calochortus pulchellus* is found in a variety of locations in Mt. Diablo State Park, where it is a protected species. Although it has no legal protected status, it is listed 1B by the California Native Plant Society in its *Inventory*.

Calochortus pulchellus was the favorite flower of Willis Jepson, who is considered by many to be California's most influential botanist of the twentieth century. As such it is the emblem displayed on the *The Jepson Manual. Higher Plants of California* (Hickman 1993), the widely used flora for California.

Calochortus pulchellus

Calochortus striatus

C A L O C H O R T U S   S T R I A T U S   P A R I S H

(A L K A L I   M A R I P O S A   L I L Y)

The alkali mariposa lily is the only member of the genus with consistently striped petals. The species is restricted to alkaline, vernally wet seeps, meadows, and plains of the western Mojave Desert and the Kern Plateau. It also occurs in western-most Nevada. *Calochortus striatus* is threatened by livestock grazing, urbanization, cooption of groundwater resources, and road construction. It is not protected under the federal Endangered Species Act or by the state of California, but is listed 1B on the California Native Plant Society's *Inventory*.

Calochortus striatus

PLATE 16

Calochortus tiburonensis

CALOCHORTUS TIBURONENSIS A. J. HILL
(TIBURON MARIPOSA LILY)

The Tiburon mariposa lily is endemic to the summit of Ring Mountain, the highest point of the Tiburon Penninsula, Marin County. It is remarkable that this mariposa lily was only recently discovered by amateur botanist and local physician Dr. Robert West, and described in 1973, despite decades of serious botanical investigation in the greater San Francisco Bay area.

Calochortus tiburonensis is an unusual species, having characteristics that align it with two sections of the genus. Its chromosome number (2n = 20) and persistent basal leaf place this species in section *Calochortus*. However, its fibrous bulb-coat and non-winged capsule align this species with members of section *Cyclobothra*. It has been suggested that the species may be the product of ancient hybrid speciation, due to its morphological and geographic intermediacy.

The Tiburon mariposa lily is protected on The Ring Mountain Preserve. There, along with six other rare plant species and one rare harvestman, the preserve affords protection to a significant natural serpentinite bunchgrassland community. *Calochortus tiburonensis* is a state-listed threatened species and is found on the California Native Plant Society's *Inventory* List 1B. It was recently reclassified by the U.S. Fish and Wildlife Service and is no longer a candidate threatened species under the federal Endangered Species Act.

Calochortus tiburonensis

PLATE 17

Calochortus weedii

CALOCHORTUS WEEDII ALPH. WOOD
VAR. VESTUS PURDY

(LATE - FLOWERED MARIPOSA LILY)

The late-flowered mariposa lily is one of the most distinctive of all California's rare lilies. Petal color patterning is exceedingly intricate, with dark red wine to brown along the fringed petal margins and a light to deep olive-yellow petal interior. Variety *vestus* is one of four varieties of *Calochortus weedii*, one other of which, *C. weedii* var. *intermedius,* is also rare in California. A third variety, *C. weedii* var. *penninsularis,* is restricted to the brush-covered granite foothills near Sierra San Pedro Martin in Baja California, Mexico. The Late-flowered mariposa lily is distinguished from other varieties by its hairier petals, distinctive coloration, and more northerly distribution.

Calochortus weedii var. *vestus* is a member of subsection *Weediani* of section *Cyclobothra*. This taxonomic group includes the rare Plummer's mariposa lily (*C. plummerae*), the San Luis mariposa lily (*C. obispoensis),* and the four varieties of *C. weedii.* Subsection *weediani* is a natural group with clear intermediates in form and geographic distribution, and some putative hybridization between members (e.g., *C. plummerae* with *C. weedii* var. *intermedius).*

As the varietal designation suggests, *C. weedii* var. *vestus* is perhaps the latest blooming of all the *Calochortus* species, typically blooming in August or the last few days of July. Threats to the small, localized populations include overgrazing by cattle and urban development of its habitat. The late-flowered mariposa lily is a California Native Plant Society List 1B species.

Calochortus weedii

VAR. *vestus*

Calochortus westonii

C A L O C H O R T U S   W E S T O N I I   E A S T W O O D

(S H I R L E Y   M E A D O W S   S T A R = T U L I P)

Shirley Meadows star-tulip is a rare lily restricted to the Greenhorn Mountains of the southern Sierra Nevada. It derives its common name from Shirley Meadows, a small dry meadow in the Sequoia National Forest in which it was originally discovered. Until quite recently, *C. westonii* was known from as few as eight populations, but many new populations of *C. westoni* have been found as a result of survey efforts following an extensive wildfire in the Sequioa National Forest.

The Shirley Meadows star-tulip is a member of subsection *Eleganti* of section *Calochortus*. Subsection *Eleganti* includes many of the star-tulips including *C. monophyllus*, the widespread Pussy ears (*C. tolmiei*) and Cat's ear (*C. elegans*), among others. Although *C. westonii* was originally described as a distinct species by the California botanist Alice Eastwood, the most recent monographer of the genus, Marion Ownbey, considered it to be a variety of Beavertail grass (*C. coeruleus*), the widespread star-tulip of the central and northern Sierra Nevada. Current California botanists recognize the distinctive nature of this taxon and consider it a legitimate species in its own right.

Calochortus westonii is not protected by the state of California and was recently reclassified by the U.S. Fish and Wildlife Service so that it is no longer a candidate rare species under the federal Endangered Species Act. It is, however, a California Native Plant Society List 1B species.

Calochortus westonii

PLATE 19

Chlorogalum grandiflorum

CHLOROGALUM GRANDIFLORUM HOOVER

(RED HILLS SOAPROOT)

The Red Hills soaproot is closely related to the common and widely distributed common soaproot, *C. pomeridianum*, but the former species bears a thinner bulb coat and has shorter pedicels. *Chlorogalum grandiflorum* is restricted in distribution to serpentinite outcrops found within the shrubby or wooded foothill slopes of the central Sierra Nevada. As with many of the rare lilies of California, very little is known about the biology or life history of this rare species. Red Hills soaproot is listed 1B by California Native Plant Society.

Chlorogalum grandiflorum

PLATE 20

Chlorogalum purpureum

Camatta Canyon amole is known from only one population in a serpentinite woodland in the Los Padres National Forest near La Panza, San Luis Obispo County. This variety of *C. purpureum* typically is distinguished from the purple amole (*C. purpureum* var. *purpureum*) primarily by its smaller inflorescence. A portion of the Camatta Canyon amole population is fenced by the U.S. Forest Service and therefore protected from its most serious threat, i.e., recreational vehicular traffic. Camatta Canyon amole is a candidate for protection under the federal Endangered Species Act, listed as a rare species by the state of California, and is listed 1B by California Native Plant Society.

Chlorogalum purpureum

VAR. *reductum*

Erythronium helenae

E R Y T H R O N I U M   H E L E N A E   A P P L E G A T E

(S T .   H E L E N A   F A W N   L I L Y)

The St. Helena fawn lily is found in a dozen or more rather small populations in dry serpentinite woodlands on the slopes of Mt. St. Helena in Napa and Sonoma Counties. *Erythronium helenae* is distinguished from other *Erythronium* species by the unique combination of mottled leaves, white perianth, yellow anthers, and its limited and distinct distribution. Because of its great beauty, this rare lily currently is threatened by horticultural collecting, as well as by local geothermal development and road construction. St. Helena fawn lily is afforded no legal protection but is on the California Native Plant Society's *Inventory* List 4.

Erythronium helenae

PLATE 22

Erythronium tuolumnense

ERYTHRONIUM TUOLUMNENSE
APPLEGATE

(TUOLUMNE FAWN LILY)

The Tuolumne fawn lily differs from several other rare lilies in having uniformly green leaves, a bulb-bearing habit, and the comparative ease with which it can be cultivated. *Erythronium tuolumnense* is found in open woodlands in the Sierra Nevada foothills of Tuolumne County. The most serious threat to existing populations is the logging of its forest habitat. The California Native Plant Society lists this species as 1B. The state of California does not provide legal protection for this rare fawn lily.

Erythronium tuolumnense

PLATE 23

Fritillaria agrestis

FRITILLARIA AGRESTIS E. GREENE

(STINKBELLS)

Fritillaria agrestis is commonly called stinkbells because of the rather unpleasant odor given off by its flowers. This *Fritillaria* species is infrequently encountered, although the genus is one of the more widespread of California's lilies. Stinkbells are restricted to low depressions in heavy soils of the chaparral and grasslands within the central portion of the California. *Fritillaria agrestis* is on the California Native Plant Society's *Inventory* List 4.

Fritillaria agrestis

PLATE 24

Fritillaria ojaiensis

FRITILLARIA OJAIENSIS A. DAVIDSON
(OJAI FRITILLARIA)

Ojai fritillaria is known from less than five populations and is restricted to rocky slopes and river basins throughout San Luis Obispo, Santa Barbara, and Ventura counties. It is rarely encountered in the wild, however, with populations rare and sporadic within this three county region. *Fritillaria ojaiensis* appears to be closely related to the Checker lily (*F. affinis*), but it is distinguished from the latter species by its darkly-speckled, dull green-yellow perianth, elliptic nectary shape, and limited distribution. Little more is known about the Ojai fritillary. *Fritillaria ojaiensis* can be found on the California Native Plant Society's *Inventory* List 1B.

Fritillaria ojaiensis

PLATE 25

Fritillaria pluriflora

FRITILLARIA PLURIFLORA BENTHAM

(ADOBE LILY)

The adobe lily is a rare species of the interior portions of the North Coast Ranges, edges of the Sacramento Valley, north central Sierra Nevada foothills, and southern Oregon. Although its geographic distribution is relatively broad among California's lilies, *F. pluriflora* is considered rare and continues to decline from habitat degradation by recreational vehicular traffic, cattle grazing, and particularly by horticultural collecting, in part because this fritillary can be grown relatively easily.

As its name suggests, the adobe lily is restricted to the heavy clay ("adobe") soils of the interior foothills of California. It is not protected by the state of California, but is found on List 1B of the California Native Plant Society's *Inventory*.

Fritillaria pluriflora

PLATE 26

Fritillaria purdyi

FRITILLARIA PURDYI EASTWOOD

(PURDY'S FRITILLARIA)

Purdy's fritillaria is a rather uncommon California lily generally restricted to serpentinite ridges in chaparral and grasslands of northwestern California. Very little is known about *Fritillaria purdyi*, but its populations are being carefully watched as a California Native Plant Society List 4 species.

Fritillaria purdyi

Fritillaria roderickii

F R I T I L L A R I A R O D E R I C K I I K N I G H T

(R O D E R I C K ' S F R I T I L L A R I A)

Roderick's fritillaria is one of the rarest of all fritillaries, being known from fewer than ten populations in Mendocino County. In addition, its taxonomic status is in question, as the new *Jepson Manual* (Hickman 1993) does not recognize this rare lily as a legitimate species. Rather, Roderick's fritillaria is considered a synonym of *F. biflora* var. *biflora*, while the U.S. Fish and Wildlife Service considers *F. roderickii* under the name *F. grayana*. Further study is need to clarify the taxonomic confusion over the distinction of this highly restricted taxon. Despite the disagreement over the taxonomic integrity of Roderick's fritillary, it is listed as a California state endangered species and appears on List 1B of the California Native Plant Society's *Inventory*.

Fritillaria roderickii

PLATE 28

Fritillaria striata

FRITILLARIA STRIATA EASTWOOD

(STRIPED ADOBE LILY)

The striped adobe lily is a rare fritillary known from less than twenty occurrences in the Greenhorn Mountains of Kern and Tulare Counties. This threatened species is distinguished by the combination of a slightly divided style, white perianth segments that are often tinged red or pink and that are generally curved at the tips, and fragrant flowers. As is true for many species in Southern California, *Fritillaria striata* is threatened with habitat loss through citriculture and urbanization, and habitat degradation through cattle grazing. The striped adobe lily is a proposed threatened species under the federal Endangered Species Act, a state-listed threatened species, and a California Native Plant Society List 1B species.

Fritillaria striata

PLATE 29

Lilium bolanderi

LILIUM BOLANDERI S. WATSON

(BOLANDER'S LILY)

Bolander's lily is a rare species with small, nodding, tubular flowers resembling an open trumpet. It is typically found on the serpentinic chaparral and lower montane coniferous forests of Del Norte, Humbolt, Mendocino, and Siskiyou Counties, and in Oregon as well. Bolander's lily is primarily pollinated by hummingbirds, but bees can occasionally be seen at its flowers. In addition, many of our western *Lilium* species are interfertile. *Lilium bolanderi*, for example, is known to hybridize with all species of the *Lilium pardalinum* complex, *L. rubescens*, and *L. washingtonianum* ssp. *purpurascens*. Although Bolander's lily is exceptionally beautiful, it is rarely seen in cultivation, in part because of its recalcitrant nature. Bolander's lily is on the CNPS *Inventory* List 4.

Lilium bolanderi

PLATE 30

Lilium humboldtii

LILIUM HUMBOLDTII ROEZL & LEICHTLIN

(HUMBOLDT LILY)

As currently recognized, the Humboldt lily is represented by two subspecies: *L. humboldtii* ssp. *humboldtii* as depicted in Plate 30, and *L. humboldtii* ssp. *ocellatum*, the ocellated lily. *Lilium humboldtii* ssp. *humboldtii* is an uncommon species of the yellow pine forests of the high Sierra Nevada and Cascade Ranges, while *Lilium humboldtii* ssp. *ocellatum* is found in southwestern California. Although the Humbolt lily is rather widespread, it is sparsely distributed and uncommonly encountered. Both subspecies are pollinated primarily by large butterflies.

The Humboldt lily is a large turk's cap lily, distinguished from other western large turk's caps by its overall larger flowers and fruits, and its bulb scale morphology. The ocellated lily differs from the Humbolt lily in its distal red spots being a lighter red near the margin, the often purplish bulb scales being crimpled or barely segmented, and its southern, more coastal distribution. Neither subspecies of *Lilium humboldtii* is protected by the state, but both are on the California Native Plant Society's *Inventory* List 4.

Lilium humboldtii

PLATE 31

Lilium maritimum

LILIUM MARITIMUM KELLOGG

(COAST LILY)

The coast lily bears small, red, tubular flowers that are somewhat bell-shaped. This rare lily is restricted to coastal prairies, scrub, fens, or gaps in the closed-cone forests in the southern counties of the North Coast Ranges. Both hummingbirds and bumblebees pollinate the Coast lily. Unlike the Humboldt lilies, however, the coast lily is rather easily grown in cultivation. *Lilium maritimum* is not afforded state or federal protection, but is on the California Native Plant Society's *Inventory* List 1B. Current threats to this species include horticultural collecting as well as loss of genetic integrity through interspecific hybridization with *L. pardalinum*.

Lilium maritimum

PLATE 32

Lilium occidentale

L I L I U M   O C C I D E N T A L E   P U R D Y

(W E S T E R N   L I L Y)

Western lily is one of the most endangered of California's (and Oregon's) *Lilium* species. It is restricted to seeps and bogs of the coastal prairie, scrub, and coniferous forests of Del Norte and Humboldt counties of California and adjacent Oregon. The small turk's cap flowers of *Lilium occidentale* are pollinated exclusively by hummingbirds. Although this rare *Lilium* is threatened with habitat development, grazing, and horticultural collecting, it can be grown successfully in cultivation.

Western lily is a state-listed endangered plant species and on List 1B of the California Native Plant Society's *Inventory*. It was recently reclassified by the U.S. Fish and Wildlife Service and is no longer a federal candidate endangered species.

Lilium occidentale

Lilium pitkinense

L I L I U M   P I T K I N E N S E   B E A N E   &   V O L L M E R
(P I T K I N   M A R S H   L I L Y)

The Pitkin Marsh lily is known from only two populations near Sebastopol, Sonoma County. Most of its wetland habitat, Pitkin Marsh, has been destroyed, and in addition, this species is threatened by horticultural collecting, competition from non-native plant species, and grazing by domestic livestock.

Lilium pitkinense currently is considered a distinct species. However, recent, unpublished taxonomic work suggests that the Pitkin Marsh lily is a subspecies of the exceptionally variable Leopard lily complex (*L. pardalinum* sspp.). The Pitkin Marsh lily is distinguished from other infraspecific taxa of *Lilium pardalinum* by its smaller perianth segments, elliptic leaves, red to orange-brown pollen, magenta anthers, and generally two-segmented bulb scales. *Lilium pitkinense* is a proposed endangered species under the federal Endangered Species Act, listed as a state endangered species, and is on the CNPS *Inventory* List 1B.

Lilium pardalinum

SSP. *pitkinense*

Lilium vollmeri

L I L I U M   V O L L M E R I   E A S T W O O D

(V O L L M E R ' S   L I L Y)

Vollmer's lily is one of five taxa of the *Lilium pardalinum* complex. Like the closely related species *L. pitkinense*, it is distinguished by its smaller perianth segments and distinctly linear (not elliptic) leaves. Vollmer's lily is restricted to *Darlingtonia* bogs as well as streamsides and springs of the Klamath Region, including southern coastal Oregon. In western Siskiyou County, it is known to form hybrid swarms with another of the leopard lily complex, *L. wigginsii*. Vollmer's lily is somewhat more common than the Pitkin Marsh lily, given its greater geographic range, but unlike the Pitkin Marsh lily, it is not easily grown in cultivation.

Lilium vollmeri is a List 4 species in the *Inventory* by the California Native Plant Society.

Lilium pardalinum

VAR. *vollmeri*

Nolina interrata

(D E H E S A   N O L I N A)

The Dehesa nolina is found at approximately ten locations in Southern California where its habitat is characterized as gabbroic or serpentinite chaparral in San Diego County and northwestern Baja California, Mexico. *Nolina interrata* bears a stem that branches underground, producing a platform of rosettes—a characteristic that places this species in Section *Arborescentes* of the genus *Nolina*. The inflorescence ascends several feet above the basal rosette and bears small, white flowers. *Nolina interrata* resembles N. *parryi* in its leaf morphology, but differs from this more common species by its somewhat larger and indehiscent fruits. Little else is known about this desert species.

Nolina interrata is a proposed threatened species under the federal Endangered Species Act and a state-listed endangered species. It also appears on the California Native Plant Society's *Inventory* List 1B. While it is afforded some protection, the Dehesa nolina is seriously threatened with residential development of its habitat and by horticultural collecting.

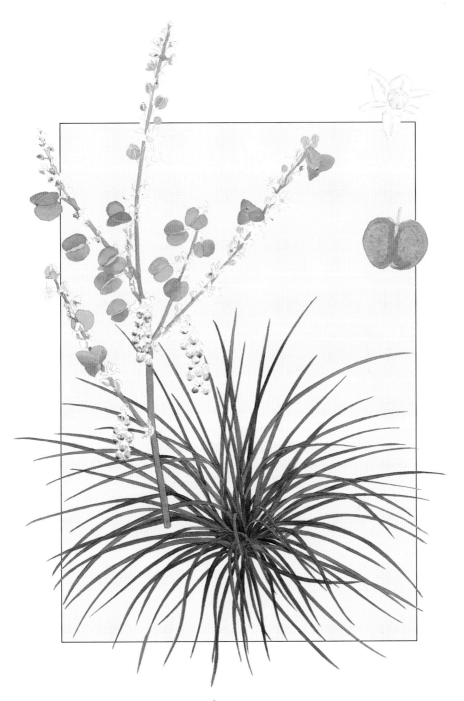

Nolina interrata

PLATE 36

Trillium rivale

(BROOK WAKEROBIN)

Brook wakerobin currently is considered uncommon in California, although this designation should be carefully reassessed when more is known about its geographic distribution. It is a species found along rocky streambanks in the yellow pine forests of the Klamath Plateau. *Trillium rivale* is distinguished from other *Trillium* species in California by its stalked flowers, petioled leaves, and nodding flowers with purple-spotted petals. It is afforded no legal protection in the state of California.

Trillium rivale

PLATE 37

Triteleia crocea

TRITELEIA CROCEA (ALPH. WOOD)
E. GREENE VAR. CROCEA

(YELLOW TRITELEIA)

Yellow triteleia is a cormous perennial found on granitic or serpentinic substrates in northern California and Oregon. This rare lily prefers the light shade of open coniferous forests of the Klamath Region, primarily at altitudes ranging from 1200 to 2000 meters. Interestingly, its flowers can also be pale blue like its sister variety, the Trinity Mountains triteleia (*T. c.* var. *modesta*), another rare species in California. These two taxa can be distinguished from each other, however, by their geographic distribution and by the degree of the fringing of the petals. The great morphological variation found in *Triteleia crocea* suggest that this rare taxon is in need of taxonomic clarification. Both *Triteleia crocea* var. *crocea* and *Triteleia crocea* var. *modesta* are listed on the California Native Plant Society's *Inventory* List 4.

Triteleia crocea

VAR. *crocea*

PLATE 38

Veratrum fimbriatum

VERATRUM FIMBRIATUM A. GRAY
(FRINGED FALSE HELLEBORE)

Veratrum fimbriatum, fringed false hellebore, is an uncommon plant of the wet meadows in the North Coast Ranges. This rare lily prefers meadows nestled in the coastal scrub of Mendocino and Sonoma Counties at approximately one hundred meters elevation. Fringed false hellebore is distinguished from all other false hellebore species in the state by its deeply fringed petals. *Veratrum fimbriatum* is placed on the California Native Plant Society's *Inventory* list 4, but is considered too common for listing by state and federal governments.

Veratrum fimbriatum

Selected References

The references listed below include all those cited in the text, as well as those more general to the study of rare plants. This listing is not an exhaustive bibliography of the California flora nor of the Liliaceae.

Allen, G.A. and J.A. Antos. 1988. Morphological and ecological variation across a hybrid zone between *Erythronium oregonum* and *E. revolutum* (Liliaceae). *Madroño* 35:32-38.

Applegate, E.I. 1935. The genus *Erythronium*: A taxonomic and distributional study of the western North American species. *Madroño* 3:58-113.

Ballantyne, O. 1978. North American lilies: let's take a closer look. *North American Lily Society Yearbook* 12:10-16.

Baker, J.G. 1873. A classified synonymic list of all the known lilies, with their native countries, and references to the works where they are figured. *Journal of the Royal Horticultural Society (New Series)* 4:39-48.

Beal, J.M. and M. Ownbey. 1943. Cytological studies in relation to the classification of the genus *Calochortus*. III. *Botanical Gazette* 104:553-562.

Beetle, D.E. 1944. A monograph of the North American species of *Fritillaria*. *Madroño* 5:133-159.

Brandt, R.P. 1916. Notes on the Californian species of *Trillium* L. III. Seasonal changes in *Trillium* species with special reference to the reproductive tissues. *University of California Publications in Botany* 7:39-68.

Cave, M.S. 1942. Development of the female gametophyte in *Erythronium helenae* and *Erythronium tuolumnense*. *Madroño* 6:177-181.

_____. 1966. The chromosomes of *Scoliopus* (Liliaceae). *Madroño* 18:211-213.

_____. 1970. Chromosomes of the California Liliaceae. *University of California Publications in Botany* 57:1-58.

Chickering, A.L. 1938. Growing *Calochortus*. *Rancho Santa Ana Monograph* 1:1-17.

Comber, A.L. 1973. A new classification of the genus *Lilium*. *Royal Horticultural Society Lily Yearbook* 13:86-105.

Dahlgren, R.M.T. and H.T. Clifford.1982. *The Monocotyledons. A Comparative Study*. New York: Academic Press.

_____, H.T. Clifford, and P.F. Yeo.1985. *The Families of the Monocotyledons*. Berlin: Springer-Verlag.

_____ and F.N. Rasmussen.1983. Monocotyledon evolution. *Evolutionary Biology* 16:255-395.

Davis, J.S. 1956. *Natural pollination of California lilies.* M.S. thesis, Claremont Graduate School, Claremont, California.

Denison, S.S. and D.W. McNeal. 1989. A re-evaluation of the *Allium sanbornii* (Alliaceae) complex. *Madroño* 36:122-130.

Drury, W.H. 1974. Rare species. *Biological Conservation* 6:162-169.

_____. 1980. Rare species of plants. *Rhodora* 82:3-48.

Eastwood, A. 1937. Quest for lilies. *Leaflets of Western Botany* 2:27-30.

_____. 1948a. Studies of Pacific Coast lilies - I. *Leaflets of Western Botany* 5:103-104.

_____. 1948b. Studies of Pacific Coast lilies - II. *Leaflets of Western Botany* 5:120-122.

_____. 1948c. Studies of Pacific Coast lilies - III. *Leaflets of Western Botany* 5:133-138.

Elwes, H.J. 1877-1880. A monograph of the genus *Lilium*. London, England.

Farwig, S. and V. Girard. 1987. *Calochortus raichei*, a new species from California. *Herbertia* 43: 2-9.

Fiedler, P.L. 1985. An investigation into the nature of rarity in the genus *Calochortus* Pursh (Liliaceae). Ph.D. dissertation, University of California, Berkeley.

_____. 1985. Heavy metal accumulation and the nature of edaphic endemism in the genus *Calochortus* Pursh (Liliaceae). *American Journal of Botany* 72:1712-1718.

_____. 1986. Concepts of rarity in vascular plant species, with special reference to the genus *Calochortus* Pursh (Liliaceae). *Taxon* 35:502-518.

_____. 1987. Life history and population dynamics of rare and common mariposa lilies (*Calochortus*: Liliaceae). *Journal of Ecology* 75:977-995.

_____ and J.J. Ahouse. 1992. Hierarchies of cause: Toward an understanding of rarity in vascular plant species. In *Conservation Biology: The Theory and Practice of Nature Conservation, Preservation, and Management.* Eds. P.L. Fiedler and S.K. Jain. New York: Chapman and Hall. 23-47.

_____ and R.K. Zebell. 1995. Two new combinations in *Calochortus clavatus* (Liliaceae). *Madroño* 42(3): 406.

Fukuda, I. and R.B. Channell. 1975. Distribution and evolutionary significance of chromosome variation in *Trillium ovatum*. *Evolution* 29:257-266.

Freeman, J.D. Revision of *Trillium* subgenus *Phyllantherum* (Liliaceae). *Brittonia* 27:1-62.

Gentry, H.S. 1946. A new *Nolina* from Southern California. *Madroño* 6:179-183.

Goodspeed, T.H. 1917. Notes on the Californian species of *Trillium* L. IV. Teratological variations of *Trillium sessile* var. *giganteum* H. & A. *University of California Publications in Botany* 7:69-100.

_____ and R.P. Brandt. 1916a. Notes on the Californian species of *Trillium* L. I. A report of the general results of field and garden studies, 1911-1916. *University of California Publications in Botany* 7:1-14.

_____ and _____. 1916b. Notes on the Californian species of *Trillium* L. II. The nature and occurrence of undeveloped flowers. *University of California Publications in Botany* 7:25-38.

Greene, E.L. 1886. Studies in the botany of California and parts adjacent. I. Some genera which have been confused under the name *Brodiaea*. *Bulletin of the California Academy [of Sciences]* 2:143-144.

_____. 1892. Notes on *Brodiaea* and *Fritillaria*. *Pittonia* 2:249-251.

Harper, J.L. 1981. The meanings of rarity. In *The Biological Aspects of Rare Plant Conservation*. Ed. H. Synge. New York: John Wiley & Sons. 189-201.

Hickman, J. ed. 1993. *Jepson Manual: Higher Plants of California*. Berkeley: University of California Press.

Hill, A.J. 1973. A distinctive new *Calochortus* (Liliaceae) from Marin County, California. *Madroño* 22:100-104.

Hoover, R.F. 1937. A new California species of *Brodiaea*. *Madroño* 4:130-132.

_____. 1939a. A definition of the genus *Brodiaea*. *Bulletin of the Torrey Botanical Club* 66:161-166.

_____. 1939b. A revision of the genus *Brodiaea*. *American Midland Naturalist* 22:551-574.

_____. 1940a. A monograph of the genus *Chlorogalum*. *Madroño* 5:137-176.

_____. 1940b. The genus *Dichelostemma*. *American Midland Naturalist* 24:463-476.

_____. 1941. A systematic study of *Triteleia*. *American Midland Naturalist* 25:75-100.

_____. 1944. *Mariposa*, a neglected genus. *Leaflets of Western Botany* 4:1-4.

_____. 1955. *Bloomeria*. *Herbertia* 11:12-23.

Hutchinson, J. 1959. *The Families of Flowering Plants. Vol. II. Monocotyledons*. Oxford: Clarendon Press.

Ingraham, J. 1953. A monograph of the genera *Bloomeria* and *Muilla* (Liliaceae). *Madroño* 12:19-27.

Keator, G. 1967. Taxonomic and ecological study of the genus *Dichelostemma* (Amaryllidaceae). Ph.D. Dissertation, University of California, Berkeley.

_____. 1987. Differentiating California's *Brodiaeas*. *Fremontia* 14:20-24.

_____. 1989. The brodiaeas. *Four Seasons* 8:4-11.

_____. 1991. Studies in the genus *Dichelostemma*. *Four Seasons* 9:24-39.

_____. 1992. Blue dicks brodiaea (*Dichelostemma capitatum*): A common but problematic species. *Four Seasons* 9:31-42.

Knapp, B. 1996. Natural history and population dynamics of *Calochortus westonii*. M.A. thesis, San Francisco State University, San Francisco, California.

Kruckeberg, A.R. 1984. *California Serpentines: Flora, Vegetation, Geology, Soils, and Management Problems*. *University of California Publications in Botany* 78:1-180.

_____ and D. Rabinowitz. 1985. Biological aspects of endemism in higher plants. *Annual Review of Ecology and Systematics* 16:447-479.

Lenz, L.W. 1966. Chromosome numbers in the Allieae (Liliaceae). *Aliso* 6:81-82.

_____. 1971. Experimental evidence for hybrid origin of *Dichelostemma venustum* (Liliaceae). *Aliso* 7:309-312.

_____. 1974. A new species of *Dichelostemma* (Liliaceae) from California. *Aliso* 8:129-131.

_____. 1975a. A biosystematic study of *Triteleia* (Liliaceae). I. Revision of the species of section *Calliprora*. *Aliso* 8:221-258.

_____. 1975b. The chromosomes of *Bloomeria* and *Muilla* (Liliaceae) and range extensions for *Muilla coronata* and *M. transmontana*. *Aliso* 8:259-262.

MacFarlane, R.M. 1978. On the taxonomic status of *Fritillaria phaeanthera* Eastw. (Liliaceae). *Madroño* 25:93-100.

Mason, H.L. 1946a. The edaphic factor in narrow endemism. I. The nature of environmental influences. *Madroño* 8:209-226.

_____. 1946b. The edaphic factor in narrow endemism. II. The geographic occurrence of plants of highly restricted patterns of distribution. *Madroño* 8:241-257.

McNeal, D.W. 1987. *Allium shevockii* (Alliaceae), a new species from the crest of the southern Sierra Nevada, California. *Madroño* 34:150-154.

_____. 1992a. A reappraisal of *Allium cristatum* (Alliaceae) and its allies. *Madroño* 39:83-89.

_____. 1992b. A revision of the *Allium fimbriatum* (Alliaceae) complex. *Aliso* 13:411-426.

Mortola, W.R. and D.W. McNeal. 1985. Taxonomy of the *Allium tribracteatum* (Alliaceae) complex. *Aliso* 11:27-35.

Mulford, A.I. 1896. *The Agaves of the United States*. Missouri Botanical Garden Annual Report 7:47-100 + Plates 26-63.

Munz, P.A. 1968. *A California Flora with Supplement*. In collaboration with D.D. Keck. Berkeley: University of California Press.

_____. 1974. *A Flora of Southern California*. Berkeley: University of California Press.

_____ and J.C. Roos. 1950. California miscellany II. *Aliso* 2:217-238.

_____ and R.F. Thorne. 1973. A new northern California *Trillium*. *Aliso* 8:15-17.

Ness, B.D. 1989. Seed morphology and taxonomic relationships in *Calochortus* (Liliaceae). *Systematic Botany* 14:495-505.

_____. 1992. Systematics and evolution of *Calochortus* (Liliaceae) with special emphasis on subsection *Nudi*. Ph.D. dissertation, Washington State University, Pullman.

_____, D.E. Soltis and P.S. Soltis. 1987. Isozyme number and allozyme differentiation in *Calochortus* subsection *Nudi* (Liliaceae). *American Journal of Botany* 74:747-748.

_____, _____ and _____. 1990. An examination of polyploidy and putative introgression in *Calochortus* subsection *Nudi* (Liliaceae). *American Journal of Botany* 77:1519-1531.

Niehaus, T.F. 1971. A biosystematic study of the genus *Brodiaea* (Amaryllidaceae). *University of California Publications in Botany* 60:1-66.

Ownbey, M. 1940. A monograph of the genus *Calochortus*. *Annals of the Missouri Botanical Garden* 27:371-561.

Painter, J.H. 1911. A revision of the subgenus *Cyclobothra* of the genus *Calochortus*. *Contributions to the U.S. National Herbarium* 13:343-350.

Parish, S.B. 1902. The southern California species of *Calochortus*. *Bulletin of the Southern California Academy of Sciences* August/November 1902:3-13.

Piper, C.V. 1916. Notes on Quamasia [=*Camassia*] with a description of a new species. *Proceedings of the Biological Society of Washington* 29:77-82.

Purdy, C. 1901. A revision of the genus *Calochortus*. *Proceedings of the California Academy of Sciences (Botany)* 2:107-158.

Rabinowitz, D. 1981. Sevens forms of rarity. In *The Biological Aspects of Rare Plant Conservation*. Ed. H. Synge. New York: John Wiley & Sons. 205-217.

Raven, P.H. and D.I. Axelrod. 1978. Origin and relationships of the California flora. *University of California Publications in Botany* 72:1-134.

Schemske, D.W., R.C. Husband, M.H. Ruckelshaus, C. Goodwille, I.M. Parker, and J.G. Bishop. 1994. Evaluating approaches to the conservation of rare and endangered plants. *Ecology* 75:584-606.

Shevock, J.R. 1984. Redescription and distribution of *Muilla coronata* (Liliaceae). *Aliso* 10:621-627.

_____, J.A. Bartel, and G.A. Allen. 1990. Distribution, ecology, and taxonomy of *Erythronium* (Liliaceae) in the Sierra Nevada of California. *Madroño* 37:261-273.

Skinner, M.W. 1988. Comparative pollination ecology and floral evolution in Pacific Coast *Lilium*. Ph.D. Dissertation, Harvard University, Cambridge, Massachusetts.

_____ and B. Pavlik. 1994. *Inventory of Rare and Endangered Vascular Plants of California.* California Native Plant Society Special Publication No. 1. Sacramento: California Native Plant Society.

Stebbins, G.L., Jr. 1942. The genetic approach to rare and endemic species. *Madroño* 6: 241-272.

_____ and J. Major. 1965. Endemism and speciation in the California flora. *Ecological Monographs* 35:1-35.

Sterling, C. 1944. On the shoot apex of *Chlorogalum pomeridianum* (DC.) Kunth. *Madroño* 7:188-192.

Stern, W.T. 1986. *Nothoscordum gracile,* the correct name of *N. fragrans* and the *N. odorum* of authors (Alliaceae). *Taxon* 35(2): 335-338.

Stoker, F. 1943. *A Book of Lilies.* The King Penguin Books, London, England and New York, New York.

Stone, E.C. 1951. The stimulative effect of fire on the flowering of the golden *Brodiaea* (*B. ixioides* var. *lugens*). *Ecology* 32:534-537.

Utech, F.H. 1979. Floral vascular anatomy of *Scoliopus bigelovii* Torrey (Liliaceae-Pardideae = Trilliaceae) and tribal note. *Annals of Carnegie Museum* 48:43-71.

Watson, S. 1879. Revision of the North American Liliaceae. *Proceedings of the American Academy of Arts and Science* 14:213-288.

Waugh, F.A. 1899. A conspectus of the genus *Lilium. Botanical Gazette* 27:235-254.

Webber, J.M. 1953. *Yuccas of the Southwest.* U.S. Department of Agriculture, Agricultural Monograph No. 17. U.S. Government Printing Office, Washington, D.C.

_____. 1960. Hybridization and instability of *Yucca. Madroño* 16:187-192.

Willis, J.C. 1973. *A Dictionary of the Flowering Plants and Ferns.* 8th ed. (Revised by H.K. Airy Shaw). Cambridge: Cambridge University Press.

Woodcock, H.B.D. and W.T. Stearn. 1950. *Lilies of the World (Their Cultivation and Classification)*. Country Life Limited, London, England and Charles Scribners Sons, New York, New York.

Zedler, P.H. and J.E. Keeley. 1973. A second location for *Nolina interrata* Gentry (Agavaceae). *Madroño* 22: 214.

Zebell, R.K. 1993. A systematic reevaluation of three species of *Calochortus* (Liliaceae): *C. venustus*, *C. simulans*, and *C. argillosus*. M.A. thesis, San Francisco State University, San Francisco, California.

_____ and P.L. Fiedler. 1992. A new combination in *Calochortus* (Liliaceae). *Madroño* 39:1991-1992.

Zomlefer, W.B. 1994. *Plant Families*. University of North Carolina Press, Chapel Hill.

Glossary

Apoendemic—geographically-restricted polyploid species descended from a more widespread ancestor of a smaller chromosomal complement

Binomial—two word scientific designation, in Latin, of a species

Bulb—underground stem characterized by thickened, fleshy scales

Bulbiferous—bearing small bulbs

California Endangered Species Act (CESA)—state law enacted in 1984 that mandates that deserving plant and animal species be given protection by the state because of their ecological, educational, historical, recreational, aesthetic, economic, and scientific value to the people of the state of California.

Rare—designation afforded by the CESA allowing that a species, ". . . although not presently threatened with extinction, [it] is in such small numbers throughout its range that it may be come endangered if its present environment worsens"

Threatened—designation afforded by the CESA allowing that a species, ". . . although not presently threatened with extinction, [it] is likely to become an endangered species in the foreseeable future in the absence of the special protection and management efforts . . ."

Endangered—designation afforded by the CESA allowing that a species is endangered when "its prospects of survival and reproduction are in immediate jeopardy from one or more causes"

Candidate—designation afforded by the CESA allowing that a species has been officially noticed by the California Department of Fish and Game Commission as being under review for addition to the rare, threatened, or endangered species lists

California Environmental Quality Act (CEQA)—state of California legislation passed in 1970 that directs all government agencies to consider the environmental impacts of projects and to avoid or mitigate where possible

California Native Plant Society (CNPS)—society of lay and professional botanists whose primary focus is the conservation, protection, and management of the California flora through education and research

> *List 1A*—list that includes all plant taxa presumed extinct within the state of California

> *List 1B*—list that includes all plant taxa rare, threatened, or endangered in the state of California and elsewhere

List 2—list that includes all plant taxa rare, threatened, or endangered in the state of California but more common elsewhere

List 3—list that includes all plant taxa about which the CNPS requests more information; a "review list"

List 4—list that includes all plant taxa of an inherently limited distribution, and to which their vulnerability or susceptibility to extinction is low; a "watch list"

Canonical Analysis—a type of statistical ordination analysis in which group means are represented by points in a multidimensional space, such that natural groups can be recognized within that space

Capsule—dry, dehiscent fruit consisting of more than one carpel

Carpel—a simple pistil formed from one modified leaf

Caudex—short, often woody, typically erect stem at or below ground level

Chromosome—a linear nuclear body composed primarily of DNA and proteins comprising a gene sequence; a unit of heredity

Chromosome Complement—the number of chromsomes in a cell nucleus

Circumboreal—distributed around the higher latitudes of the Northern Hemisphere

Contractile Roots—roots produced by an underground stem that, by various mechanisms of contraction, move the underground organ, typically a bulb or corm, downward through the soil profile

Corm—a short, solid, vertical underground stem

Cyme—a flat-topped or rounded inflorescence in which the terminal (distal) flower blooms first

Dioecions—condition when flowers are unisexual and borne on separate individuals

Endangered Species Act (ESA)—federal legislation enacted in 1977, and amended since, to protect various species of fish, wildlife, and plants in the United States. The ESA is administered by the U.S. Fish and Wildlife Service (USFWS) and the National Marine Fisheries Service (NMFS)

Endangered Species—any species, including a subspecies, that is "in danger of extinction throughout all or a significant portion of its range"

Threatened Species—any taxon that is "likely to become an endangered species within the foreseeable future within all or a significant portion of its range"

Proposed Species—any endangered or threatened taxon for which a proposed regulation but not a final rule has been published in the *Federal Register*

Epithet—the second name of a Latin binomial in the science of taxonomy

Exotic—non-native; foreign; often used referring to an organism that has been introduced into an area

Genus (pl. Genera)—rank in the taxonomic hierarchy forming the principal category between that of the family and the species

Infraspecific—below the level of the species, e.g., variety, subspecies, etc.

Intraspecific—within a single species

Interspecific—between two or more species

Liliaceae—large plant family of the class Monocotyledonae

Monochasial—bearing a type of cymose inflorescence with a single main axis

Monoecions—condition when flowers are unisexual and borne on the same individual

Native—indigenous to an area

Native Plant Protection Act (NPPA)—state of California legislation passed in 1977 that directs the California Department of Fish and Game (CDFG) to carry out the state legislature's intent to "preserve, protect and enhance endangered plants in this State," effectively empowering the CDFG Commission to designate native plants as endangered, rare, or threatened, and to require permits for the collection of, transportation of, or selling of such plants

Neoendemic—newly evolved species of limited distribution

Paleoendemic—very old species, often but not always of limited distribution

Patroendemic—diploid species of limited distribution that presumably gave rise to a younger, more widespread, polyploid species

Pedicel—flower stalk or stem

Perianth—the two leaf-like outer whorls of a flower; collectively the petals and sepals

Phylogeny—evolutionary history of a lineage

Polycarpic—flowering more than once during the lifetime of a plant

Polyploid—having greater than two sets of homologous chromosomes

Population—group of individuals of the same species occupying a specific area and typically isolated at least somewhat from other like groups

Principal Component Analysis—a statistical method of transforming any multidimensional space in which observations occur such that the first axis explains the maximum amount of variance, the second (orthogonal to the first) axis explains the maximum amount of the remaining variance, and so on.

Rarity—condition of geographic distribution and population abundance that is typically characterized by either few individuals, a small geographic range, or both

   Natural Rarity—a taxon that is rare due solely to its biology, evolutionary history, or both

   Anthropogenic Rarity—a taxon that is rare due primarily or solely to negative interactions with humans; taxon may have been naturally rare before it declined due to anthropogenic causes

Relictual—having survived from a past geologic epoch

Schizoendemic—descendent taxon that bears the same number of chromosomes as its parent species; the splitting of taxa can occur rapidly or not

Serpentinite—a mineral characterized by the presence of toxic metals, e.g., chromium, nickel, aluminum, as well as the presence of large, sometimes toxic amounts of magnesium and a paucity of calcium

Staminode (pl. staminodia)—sterile stamen(s)

Taxon (pl. taxa)—taxonomic group or unit, including all other subordinate groups

Tepal—condition of perianth when sepals are not differentiated from the petals, appearing identical

U.S. Fish and Wildlife Service (USFWS)—federal agency within the Department of Interior whose responsibility, among others, is to oversee the implementation and enforcement of the Endangered Species Act

Appendix A

between the Liliaceae and several monocot families now segregated but
traditionally included in the Liliaceae

Character	Liliaceae	Agavaceae
Representative Genera	*Calochortus, Erythronium, Fritillaria, Lilium, Tulipa*	*Agave, Yucca*
Distribution	mostly temperate Northern Hemisphere	Subtropical to tropical regions
Habit	Perennial herbs: bulbs or seldom rhizomes	Large, perennial herbs to tree-like, with secondary growth; rhizomes
Leaf Position	Cauline or basal	Dense apical rosettes
Inflorescence	Racemose, unbellate, or flower solitary	Racemose or paniculate; large
Perianth Differentiation	Tepals; showy, often spotted	Tepals; showy
Perianth Fusion	Distinct	Distinct or fused at base
Fruit Type	Capsule, rarely a berry	Capsule or sometimes a berry
Seed shape	Flat or rounded	Usually flat

Modified and adapted from Zomlefer (1994).

Alliaceae	Asparagaceae	Dracaenaceae	Trilliaceae
Allium, Brodiaea, Muilla, Nothoscordum	*Maianthemum, Smilacina*	*Nolina*	*Trillium*
Widely distributed	Northern Hemisphere & Old World tropics, with a few in South America	Tropical to subtropical regions	Mostly Northern Hemisphere
Perennial herbs: bulbs	Perennial herbs, vines or shrubs: rhizomes	Large, perennial herbs to tree-like, with secondary growth; rhizomes	Perennial: herbs rhizomes
Basal rosettes	Cauline or in basal rosettes	Basal or apical rosettes	Cauline
Umbellate; subtended by bracts, scapose	Umbellate, racemose, or spicate	Racemose, paniculate, or umbellate	Flowers solitary
Tepals; ± showy	Tepals; usually inconspicuous	Tepals; generally showy	Often sepals and petals; showy
Distinct or fused (tubular or bell-shaped)	Distinct or fused at base	Distinct or often fused at base (tubular)	Distinct
Capsule	Usually a berry	Berry or nut-like	Berry or capsule
Tetrahedral, triagonal, or rounded	Globose	Globose to ellipsoid	Globose to ellipsoid

Appendix B

Genus	Status[1]	No. of California Taxa (N/E)[2]	No. of Rare Taxa[3]
Agave	Native	3 / 0	2
Allium	Native/Exotic	59 / 4	17
Aloe	Exotic	0 / 1	0
Androstephium	Native	1 / 0	1
Asparagus	Exotic	0 / 2	0
Asphodelus	Exotic	0 / 1	0
Bloomeria	Native	2 / 0	1
Brodiaea	Native	18 / 0	7
Calochortus	Native	51 / 0	25
Camassia	Native	2 / 0	0
Chlorogalum	Native	7 / 0	4
Clintonia	Native	2 / 0	0
Dichelostemma	Native	6 / 0	0
Disporum	Native	2 / 0	0
Erythronium	Native	14 / 0	8
Fritillaria	Native	20 / 0	13
Hastingsia	Native	2 / 0	0
Hesperocallis	Native	1 / 0	0
Ipheion	Exotic	0 / 1	0
Leucocrinum	Native	1 / 0	0
Lilium	Native	18 / 0	12
Maianthemum	Native	1 / 0	0
Muilla	Native	4 / 0	2
Muscari	Exotic	0 / 1	0
Narthecium	Native	1 / 0	0

Nolina	Native	4 / 0	1
Nothoscordum	Exotic	0 / 1	0
Odontostomum	Native	1 / 0	0
Scoliopus	Native	1 / 0	0
Smilacina	Native	2 / 0	0
Smilax	Native	2 / 0	0
Stenanthium	Native	1 / 0	0
Streptopus	Native	1 / 0	0
Tofieldia	Native	1 / 0	0
Trillium	Native	6 / 0	1
Triteleia	Native	17 / 0	5
Veratrum	Native	4 / 0	2
Xerophyllum	Native	1 / 0	0
Yucca	Native	4 / 0	0
Zigadenus	Native	7 / 0	0

[1] Status refers to whether the genus and any or all of its species is considered native to California, or exotic (i.e., non-native).

[2] N = Number of native taxa; E = Number of exotic taxa

[3] Rarity is determined according to Skinner, M.W. and B.M. Pavlik, eds. 1994. *Inventory of Rare and Endangered Vascular Plants of California.* 5th ed. California Native Plant Society, Sacramento.

Appendix C

LATIN NAME	STATE/FEDERAL STATUS[1]	CNPS STATUS[2]
Agave shawii	None	List 2
Agave utahensis	None	List 4
Allium atrorubens var. *atrorubens*	None	List 2
Allium fimbriatum var. *purdyi*	None	List 4
Allium hickmanii	None	List 1B
Allium hoffmanii	None	List 4
Allium howellii var. *clokeyi*	None	List 4
Allium munzii	CT/PE	List 1B
Allium nevadense	None	List 2
Allium parishii	None	List 4
Allium sanbornii var. *congdonii*	None	List 4
Allium sharsmithiae	None	List 1B
Allium shevockii	None	List 1B
Allium siskiyouense	None	List 4
Allium tribracteatum	None	List 1B
Allium tuolumnense	-/PT	List 1B
Allium yosemitense	CR/-	List 1B
Androstephium breviflorum	None	List 2
Bloomeria humilis	CR/-	List 1B
Brodiaea coronaria ssp. *rosea*	CE/-	List 1B
Brodiaea filifolia	CE/-	List 1B
Brodiaea insignis	CE/-	List 1B
Brodiaea kinkiensis	None	List 1B
Brodiaea orcuttii	None	List 1B

Brodiaea pallida	CE/-	List 1B
Calochortus albus var. *rubellus*	None	None
Calochortus argillosus	None	None
Calochortus catalinae	None	List 4
Calochortus clavatus var. *avius*	None	List 1B
Calochortus clavatus var. *clavatus*	None	List 4
Calochortus clavatus var. *gracilis*	None	List 1B
Calochortus clavatus var. *recurvifolius*	None	List 1B
Calochortus dunnii	CR/-	List 1B
Calochortus excavatus	None	List 1B
Calochortus greenei	None	List 1B
Calochortus longebarbatus var. *longebarbatus*	None	List 1B
Calochortus monanthus	None	List 1A
Calochortus obispoensis	None	List 1B
Calochortus palmeri var. *munzii*	None	List 1B
Calochortus palmeri var. *palmeri*	None	List 1B
Calochortus panamintensis	None	List 4
Calochortus persistens	CR/-	List 1B
Calochortus plummerae	None	List 1B
Calochortus pulchellus	None	List 1B
Calochortus raichei	None	List 1B
Calochortus simulans	None	List 4
Calochortus striatus	None	List 1B
Calochortus tiburonensis	CT/-	List 1B
Calochortus umbellatus	None	List 4
Calochortus venustus var. *sanguineus*	None	None
Calochortus weedii var. *intermedius*	None	List 1B
Calochortus weedii var. *vestus*	None	List 1B
Calochortus westonii	None	List 1B
Chlorogalum grandiflorum	None	List 1B
Chlorogalum purpureum var. *minus*	None	List 1B

Chlorogalum purpureum var. *purpureum*	None	List 1B
Chlorogalum purpureum var. *reductum*	CR/-	List 1B
Erythronium citrinum var. *citrinum*	None	List 4
Erythronium citrinum var. *roderickii*	None	List 1B
Erythronium helenae	None	List 4
Erythronium hendersonii	None	List 2
Erythronium howellii	None	List 4
Erythronium klamathense	None	List 4
Erythronium pluriflorum	None	List 1B
Erythronium pusaterii	None	List 1B
Erythronium tuolumnense	None	List 1B
Fritillaria agrestis	None	List 4
Fritillaria biflora var. *ineziana*	None	List 1B
Fritillaria brandegei	None	List 1B
Fritillaria eastwoodiae	None	List 1B
Fritillaria falcata	None	List 1B
Fritillaria lanceolata var. *tristulis*	None	List 1B
Fritillaria liliacea	None	List 1B
Fritillaria ojaiensis	None	List 1B
Fritillaria pluriflora	None	List 1B
Fritillaria purdyi	None	List 4
Fritillaria roderickii	CE/-	List 1B
Fritillaria striata	CT/-	List 1B
Fritillaria viridea	None	List 4
Lilium bolanderi	None	List 4
Lilium humboldtii ssp. *humboldtii*	None	List 4
Lilium humboldtii ssp. *ocellatum*	None	List 4
Lilium kelloggii	None	List 4
Lilium maritum	none	List 1B
Lilium occidentale	CE/-	List 1B
Lilium pitkinense	CE/-	List 1B

Lilium vollmeri	None	List 4
Lilium wigginsii	None	List 4
Lilium parryi	None	List 1B
Lilium rubescens	None	List 4
Lilium purpurascens	None	List 4
Muilla clevelandii	None	List 1B
Muilla coronata	None	List 4
Nolina interrata	CE/-	List 1B
Trillium ovatum ssp. *oettingeri*	None	List 4
Trillium rivale	None	None
Triteleia clementina	None	List 1B
Triteleia crocea var. *crocea*	None	List 4
Triteleia crocea var. *modesta*	None	List 4
Triteleia hendersonii var. *hendersonii*	None	List 2
Triteleia ixioides ssp. *cookii*	None	List 4
Veratrum fimbriatum	None	List 4
Veratrum insolitum	None	List 4

[1] None = No federal or state protection under the federal or state Endangered Species Acts; CE/ = California state-listed endangered species; CR/ = California state-listed rare species; CT/ = California state-listed threatened species; /C = Federally-listed candidate species; /PT = Federally proposed threatened; and /PE = Federally proposed endangered.

[2] California Native Plant Society List (*Inventory of Rare and Endangered Vascular Plants of California* [Skinner, M.W. and B.M. Pavlik. 1994. California Native Plant Society Special Publication 1, 5th edition, Sacramento, California]). List 1A = taxon presumed extinct; List 1B = taxon rare, threatened, or endangered throughout its range; List 2 = taxon rare, threatened, or endangered throughout California but more common elsewhere; List 3 = taxon about which more information is needed; and List 4 = taxon not currently rare, threatened, or endangered, but may soon be in danger of becoming so.

Appendix D

SEVEN FORMS OF RARITY
AS ILLUSTRATED BY
THE CALIFORNIAN LILIACEAE
(AFTER RABINOWITZ, 1979)

Geographic Range	Large	
Habitat Specificity	Wide	Narrow
	Widespread Taxa	Predictable Taxa
Large, Dominant, Local Populations	Common Plants *Allium validum*	*Calochortus striatus*
Small, Non-dominant, Local populations	Sparse Plants *Muilla coronata*	*Nolina interrata*

Geographic Range	Small	
Habitat Specificity	Wide	Narrow
	Unlikely Endemic Taxa	Endemic Taxa
Large, Dominant, Local Populations	*Allium munzii*	*Calochortus tiburonensis*
Small, Non-dominant, Local populations	Non-Existent?	*Brodiaea pallida*

PEGGY LEE FIEDLER received her undergraduate degree in ethnobotany from Harvard University (1979), and her M.A. (1980) and Ph.D. (1985) in applied plant ecology and evolution from the University of California at Berkeley. Currently, she is Associate Professor of Conservation Biology at San Francisco State University. Her research explores the biology of rare plant species, focusing primarily on the mariposa lilies (*Calochortus*). Dr. Fiedler also studies the ecology of California wetlands, with a special interest in furthering wetland conservation efforts. With several colleagues, she recently completed a classification of wetlands in the coastal watersheds of Central and Southern California. She is senior editor on two conservation biology anthologies, one published in 1992 by Chapman and Hall, and one forthcoming. Peggy lives in Oakland with her husband, Robert, son Garrett, and daughter Jena Louise.

CATHERINE M. WATTERS was born and raised in Paris where her love of art and flowers began. She moved to California as a teenager and received her B.A. in 1974 from the University of California, Davis, where she studied French literature and art. Catherine has been a botanical artist for the past ten years, painting life-size watercolors primarily from live specimens. Besides working on her numerous commissions and yearly shows, she is an avid photographer of flowers. Catherine lives in Oakland with her husband, Bob, and two sons, Christopher and David.